P9-DTF-114

JEWELRY
How to Create Your Image

To my friend Baron Francois de Berenx,
with my best wishes,

Roger Mijol.

JEWELRY
How to create your image.

Jorge Miguel
with Diane Jennings

Still-life Photography by Andy Vracin

Fashion Photography by Peter Robbins

Taylor Publishing Company
Dallas, Texas

Book Design by Alan Lidji

**Library of Congress
Cataloging-in-Publication Data**

Miguel, Jorge
  Jewelry, how to create your image.
  1. Beauty, Personal. 2. Clothing and dress.
  3. Jewelry. I. Jennings, Diane. II. Title.
  RA778.M527   1985   646   85-25070
          ISBN 0-87833-518-8

Printed in the United States of America

To the three people who actually
believed in me, Don Javier Garza Sepulveda,
Jorge Rudney Atalla, and
of course, Albert Lidji.
Special thanks to
the Summers family for
their continued friendship and support.

Table of Contents

Introduction

In my 15 years as a jeweler at two renowned specialty stores, I have worked with some of the most fascinating women in the world and with some of the most beautiful gems in the world.

Each day I spend in this time-honored profession, I become more enthralled with the challenge of matching the incomparable creations of time and nature with the personalities and physical attributes of today's woman. To me there is nothing more exciting than seeing a woman's beauty enhanced by wearing one of nature's most astounding creations, a striking stone perhaps or a priceless pearl.

Today's woman is more aware than ever before of the importance of the image she projects, and rightly so. But that image is not restricted to one part of her personality. When it comes to self-expression, image is not simply a matter of clothes or cosmetics. It is an overall impression created by putting everything together successfully — and that includes jewelry. As one of my best customers puts it: A woman without jewelry is like a sentence without punctuation!

Dress-for-success experts and color consultants are flourishing these days because everyone wants to know how to maximize his strengths and minimize his weaknesses — while still getting quality and value.

What a shame the same consideration is not given to jewelry! For years jewelry has been viewed simply as an accessory to beautiful clothes, a way to accent a chic suit or set off a gorgeous gown. What disturbs me is the amount of money people will spend on jewelry, merely as an afterthought — even though it usually costs several times the price of the clothing it is meant to complement. Conditioned to think that way, many of my clients find it difficult to share my opinion that clothes should be purchased to set off fine gems, instead of the other way around. I am stunned at the number of women who spend hundreds of dollars on an outfit, and *then* spend several thousand more on jewelry.

In all likelihood, the dress you buy today will be discarded in a few years. It will go out of style, no longer fit, show signs of wear or you may simply tire of it.

But the gems you purchase today to accessorize that dress will literally last forever. Most people acknowledge, but rarely think about, the fact that the stones you're wearing today have been in existence for millions of years. The diamond you cherish may be fresh out of the mine, or it may be a stone that has belonged to numerous owners through thousands of years. But it is always the product of millions of years of nature at work.

Like great art, we never really *own* fine gems — we simply serve as stewards until they are passed on to others. That aspect of beautiful gems never ceases to fascinate me: buildings crumble and the most beautiful oil painting fades, but the fire of a diamond or the lustre of a pearl will last long after man's other monuments to art and beauty have vanished.

And unlike the dress you select so carefully, jewelry is not subject to the whims of fashion. Certainly styles come and go, but when bought with care and thought, most jewels will remain classics. The interest shown in famous antique pieces or family heirlooms handed down from generation to generation is as strong today as in years past.

Jewelry is also not affected by slight figure changes. The earring you selected at age 25 will look just as good on your ear at age 50, while the dress you purchased in younger years will undoubtedly be hard pressed to follow normal figure changes.

Even the best clothing manufacturers do not expect their designs to stand the test of time in either durability or style indefinitely. More likely you will grow tired of the dress, and even if it has held its style, fit, and quality, after 25 years you will undoubtedly discard it in favor of something fresher. You may also tire of your jewelry, but unlike the material clothing is made of, you can redesign gems into something you like better.

To me that is one of the magical things about jewels: they are a precious commodity that not only can be used, but in most cases, *improve* with use. Taking all the factors into consideration — their initial cost, beauty, and durability — I am even more stunned at the casual method most people employ when buying jewels. Not only do they often buy their jewels *after* purchasing clothes, they usually buy without giving a thought to whether or not the jewelry will complement the outfit or their own coloring, body shape, and facial characteristics.

Women have always been aware of the small touches that improve their appearance, such as the need for big boned women to avoid large prints, and the practicality of a petite woman wearing vertical looks. Similarly in recent years, thanks in no small measure to Carole Jackson and her book, *Color Me Beautiful,* women are more aware than ever before of the importance of color, what tones highlight their features and what tones don't.

But when it comes to buying jewelry, despite the greater investment involved, these considerations tend to go out the window. Most women buy jewelry on impulse. They spy a striking piece of jewelry displayed on black velvet and take it home — then are disappointed when it doesn't look nearly as attractive on them as it did in the store. But just like clothing, certain jewelry types look good on certain body shapes, and certain colors of stones look better with certain facial and hair colors.

Most women would never consider buying a dress without taking it off the hanger, trying it on, and watching how it moves. So why buy jewelry without trying it on first, checking it in different light, and seeing how it looks with not just one but several outfits? You should note how it looks not only on your ear or hand or neck, but also how it fits into your overall appearance. Does the shape flatter your size? Is it the right color for your hair and eyes and skin or does it look washed out? Does the overall feeling of the jewelry combine well with the occasions you have in mind?

All of these questions and others deserve to be taken into account. After all, what you are doing when selecting jewelry is making a statement, expressing your personality, letting the world know who and what you are. And because the jewelry you wear will cost more and last longer than most clothes, these factors should be considered from the very beginning.

But this is not a book just for the very wealthy who can afford to buy the legendary gems of the world. This is a book for anyone wanting value for her money, anyone who prizes craftsmanship and beauty. And by value for the dollar, I mean quality, not quantity. No one should spend any amount of money on a piece that is wrong for her or a piece that is overpriced, simply because she doesn't know any better.

Anyone desiring to buy so much as one piece of jewelry should feel confident that what she is buying is an investment in pleasure as well as dollars. Acquiring fine jewelry is essentially the process of assembling a collection of wearable art. While you may not be able to afford the biggest or the best, you also cannot afford to buy something inappropriate or in bad taste. No one can afford a mistake, no matter what her financial circumstances. Any piece of jewelry that goes unworn because it was a bad buy either in quality or as it relates to the wearer is a costly mistake, regardless of the price tag.

There are no rights and wrongs, of course, but the purchase and selection of jewelry should be fun, not an experience fraught with uncertainty and risk. Yet if you buy foolishly, without any thought of the principles in this book, you run the great risk of buying jewelry that for some reason you prefer not to wear, so it spends more time out of sight than on your body.

Such mistakes are not just a personal shame, but a public tragedy. Nature requires millions of years to produce the stuff of which dazzling jewelry is made and talented artisans spend countless hours of painstaking work to display them at their best. Beautiful gems and metals deserve an appreciative audience, which is exactly what they get when worn by just the right person at just the right moment.

Knowing how to buy quality jewelry that is right for you is as important as wearing the proper suit to a business meeting or the right evening gown to that special occasion. There are few bad pieces, merely bad selections, and too many customers make purchases that are just plainly wrong for them.

Buying jewelry is an investment like no other — an investment in money, but also an investment in beauty and confidence. What you select to wear evidences not only your knowledge of fine gems, and your good taste, but ultimately your own image. The jewelry you wear is simply an extension of your own personal style. We all have our own hallmarks that express our uniqueness, and jewelry deserves to be included in that style, not added as an afterthought. It takes conscious effort to develop one's own style, but those who do are the ones we remember, whether it be the memorable star quality of a Carol Channing or the supreme self-confidence of a Diana Vreeland.

But before you analyze your personal attributes and the best way to express that uniqueness, it's necessary to take a look at the wide range of jewelry pieces made available by dedicated artisans. To me, there's nothing quite as exciting as matching these beautiful, wearable pieces of art with the fascinating women of the '80s. And once you've tried it yourself, I think you'll agree!

The color of a pearl is determined by many factors, including the food supply and mineral content of the mollusk, but the pearl always matches the lining of the shell.

Chapter One

Jewelry Styles—Ear Lobe to Fingertip

Buying jewelry can be a matter of simply walking into a jewelry store and selecting the earring, necklace, bracelet, or ring that catches your eye. But I would like to suggest that, before you so much as linger over a display case, you take a moment at home to take stock of your assets. And by "assets" I'm not referring to your bank account — I assume you've taken stock of that before deciding to purchase any jewelry at all!

Taking Stock

What I am referring to is your appearance, body type, and coloring, of course; but I also mean taking stock of your jewelry box. Gather up every piece of jewelry you have ever purchased and spread it out before you. Sift through it, and analyze what types of jewelry you have purchased in the past and why. Look at what your preferences have been in the past. Most important, set aside those pieces you not only purchased but those you also wear regularly. Ask yourself why you like those pieces, and make a mental note of your likes and dislikes. File those notes away for future reference when shopping. You may have made mistakes in the past, but you can at least profit from them.

It's critical to analyze what jewelry you've bought in the past, so you can plan what to buy in the future. The trick is to buy pieces that reflect your style, your tastes, and preferences. That way, through the years you will develop a style that is uniquely yours, instead of a collection of trendy items that will quickly become dated. That's not to say your jewelry wardrobe won't be fashionable. Like the Chanel jacket, some styles never go out of fashion — and most important of all, if it's your style, it's always in fashion.

Types of Jewelry

There are numerous types of jewelry to consider, but thankfully it's not as complicated as it once was. During the

Middle Ages, for instance, no woman of rank was considered well dressed without a large and small necklace, a brooch, large and small earrings, rings, a corsage brooch, several bracelets, and possibly a tiara. Today, however, the basic jewelry wardrobe consists of earrings, necklaces, bracelets, rings, and possibly a pin.

Head and Neck

Hair ornaments, such as tiaras, did not withstand the test of time, because they became synonymous with an outmoded class structure. Nonetheless, the first body area anyone notices is the head, and it must be properly adorned with jewelry that has aged well — earrings. I'm not the only one who feels earrings are the single most important piece of jewelry in a woman's wardrobe; in a survey of my customers, almost every woman said she felt undressed without these small but crucial pieces.

These small accessories contribute enormously to your overall image. The head is constantly moving and no one can help but notice the swing of a dangle or the tiny button clipped to your lobe.

Perhaps that explains why decorations for the ear have been popular for thousands of years. Ancient carvings show images of rulers sporting earrings, and the burial place of King Tut contained, among other fabulous treasures, a pair of earrings. Earrings were especially popular during the days of the Roman Empire, with Julius Caesar being particularly fond of them. Shakespeare has been pictured wearing an earring, and he also placed a ring in the ear of the character, Othello. But earrings for men faded from favor after Charles I of England went to his execution wearing one.

Their popularity has never faded with women, however. Large earrings were stylish as early as 4,000 years ago, and they remain in vogue around the world. From the elephant hairs the

Clip-on earrings can be just as versatile as pierced, as shown by these simple loops and elaborate diamond earrings.

African tribal woman slips through her lobes to the mismatched earrings the punk-style teenager wears on the streets of New York, earrings today are as popular and stylish as ever. Most women start wearing earrings during adolescence, though some cultures even begin adorning the ears in infancy.

There are two basic types of earrings, the pierced and the clip-on. In the U.S. the trend is unmistakably toward pierced ears. Few women make it through their teenage years without joining in what I consider an unfortunate trend. In my opinion, they would be better off without holes in their ears for several reasons.

The primary problem with pierced earrings is that they must be placed in the same spot every time. Some shapes and sizes of earrings look better placed on different areas of the ear, but a pierced earring obviously cannot be adjusted the way a clip-on can. Approach the purchase of earrings as if you were buying a miniature sculpture. Like any piece of art, it looks different from various angles. You wouldn't place a beautiful piece of art in a corner of a room just because the corner is bare. You would select the spot where it could be shown to best advantage, thus increasing your pleasure as the owner and the pleasure of those viewing it.

So why place different designs and shapes in the same spot on your earlobe, just because a hole has been drilled there? It's far better to accommodate the size and shape of your lobe with the shape of the earring, and that can only be done with clip-on earrings.

But there are other reasons I prefer clip-ons to pierced earrings, including reasons of health. Many earrings, particularly fine pieces, are heavy and may suspend enough weight on the lobe to stretch it. Because jewelry is meant to enhance beauty, not detract from it, this is an unacceptable side effect.

Although many earrings sold today are of the pierced variety, the inventory of most fine jewelers is heavily weighted

Only the very tiny ear requires pierced earrings, but if you prefer them, a wide variety from studs to buttons and dangles is available.

toward clip-ons. I do not carry pierced earrings at my salon except on special order.

The only exception to my preference for non-pierced ears is in the case of an unusually small earlobe, one so tiny as to be impossible to fit with clip-on earrings. Such lobes are very rare, and most women do not need to concern themselves with this problem.

Styles

There are several basic styles of earrings to choose from: the stud, the loop, the button, and the drop or dangle earring. The stud is a small, simple earring usually made of a solid metal or a tiny stone. The loop or hoop is a circle shape that goes under the lobe and comes in various widths, while the button is a single flat or domed round, made from metals or stones. The button is the most popular shape today, but dangle or drop earrings, those with a loose, hanging design, sometimes attached to a button or cluster, are coming back in style.

There are numerous choices to be made, but the important thing to consider is your facial and earlobe shape. This is the context in which the earring fits, the place where everyone looks. The earring should make you look good without overpowering you. It should express you at your best, and once you know what flatters your facial and earlobe shape, nothing can stop you from making a subtle but powerful personal fashion statement with that tiny piece of sculpture.

Neck and Upper Torso

Like earrings, necklaces have been worn by men and women since ancient times, usually as a symbol of power or honor. Today necklaces are worn primarily by women, and strictly as a fashion accessory. Because necklaces are often more conspicuous than other jewelry pieces, such as rings and earrings, many women are unsure of what is right for them. As a result they tend to avoid necklaces altogether, which, in my

Earring styles include the button (top), and a variation (top right), loops (bottom), and dangles (left).

opinion, is a sad statement about a woman's self-confidence. Again, a necklace is worn in that all-important head and neck area. When people meet you for the first time they look at your face — taking in those earrings — but it is only a matter of inches between the face and neck, and that neck deserves to be properly adorned.

Indeed, the neck is often a crucial area because it is more subject to changes than any other body area. Any tasteful image you project will take into account your age, and the neck ages more noticeably than almost any other area. Don't overlook the importance of dressing this area properly.

Styles

Fortunately, as with earrings, there are many necklace types to choose from. As the most obvious aspect of a necklace is its length, the traditional names of certain necklaces are derived from that aspect.

The choker is the most popular type of necklace today. It will probably continue to hold that favored spot, and for good reason: it is popular because of its versatility. Depending on the materials it is made from, a choker can be very dressy or quite casual. Also, though it is usually a short necklace that fits close to the neck, a choker's length can vary from 14 to 18 inches, depending on your facial and neck characteristics. Most chokers are made of bulky materials, and while they may consist of only one strand, more often they are multistranded. If you don't have a choker and it's appropriate for your body shape and image, I strongly recommend making this style necklace your first major purchase.

The next longest necklace is a single strand called the "princess," usually about 18 inches long. This type of necklace is not particularly popular today, probably because the length is too demure for today's woman. Today's woman is too busy, too active, to be bothered with accessories that fail to express her

The choker's popularity reflects today's preference for bold, clean lines and uncomplicated design.

personality. Because it is neither long nor short, there are few necklines that go well with the princess length.

Most women prefer the shorter choker for a dressier look or a longer strand for a more casual feel, because both say something to the viewer. Women of the '80s don't want to merely blend into the crowd, which is exactly what the princess necklace does. In the past such styles may have fit the old adage, smile-sweetly-and-keep-your-hands-in-your-lap, but that advice simply doesn't hold true today.

The matinee necklace, which is longer at 20 to 24 inches, goes well with a great many fashions. It complements the clean uncluttered lines of today's clothes without getting in the way, and is one I highly recommend.

Longer necklaces such as the opera length (28 to 36 inches) are often impractical. Women today do not simply sit still and look pretty. They are constantly on the go and don't want their activity hampered by worrying about a long necklace getting in the way.

That may be why the rope, which is an amazing 45 to 120 inches long, is considered somewhat passé today — it may have been appropriate and attractive when women were more sedentary, but for women flying between business meetings and leisure lunches, it holds little appeal.

There is one necklace that is truly a classic and that is the "riviere." Hailed as the ultimate necklace by many jewelers, a riviere is a single strand of varying length, made solely of stones, usually diamonds. The name literally means "river stream" which is exactly what it looks like: a shimmering, flowing stream of fire and light. It's been said there's no hope for the man who doesn't look good in a tuxedo, and I feel the same about a woman in a carefully chosen riviere.

When buying a necklace it is especially important to consider the clasp. Many people consider the clasp a piece of hardware that is necessary but not particularly attractive. With

Clasps are especially important to consider when buying a necklace because people view you from the back as well as the front.

truly fine jewelry, however, pieces that are crafted by artisans who take great pride in their work, clasps become an artist's signature. The clasp is not only a piece that connects one end of a necklace to the other, but an integral part of the jewelry itself.

The clasp most people are familiar with is called a "spring ring." A spring ring is a tiny circle that works with a spring mechanism to open and close for fastening. While it does the job, which is to hold the two ends of your necklace together, it is strictly functional and adds little beauty.

I much prefer a plunging clasp, in which fingers of the fastener are hidden within a decorative case. These cases often rival the center stone of the necklace in beauty, as they may include dozens of tiny but brilliant stones or extensive enamel and metal work.

Don't ignore the clasp just because it will be worn at the back of your neck. In large gatherings, people view you from the back as well as the front. When it comes to expressing yourself and presenting a put-together image, attention to such details as jewelry clasps is essential.

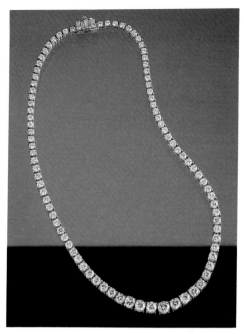

A single strand of diamonds makes a classic necklace style known as the "riviere."

Arm and Hand

Clasps can also be important when selecting a bracelet, but the most popular bracelet type today is one that has no clasp at all: the bangle. Bangles have probably been in existence since the first bracelet was formed. "Bracelet" is actually a derivation from the French word "bras" which means "arm." Bracelets were once used for functional purposes, purportedly to give warriors added strength in combat by constricting the muscles in the forearm.

Women have traditionally worn bracelets closer to the wrist, and for decorative purposes alone. The bangle, which is a stiff, circular piece that slips over the hand, is probably the most popular bracelet today because it is easy to wear and, like the choker, extremely versatile.

There are two basic bracelet styles that appear most often, the flexible (left and right) and the bangle (center).

Bangles vary in width from a quarter inch to two inches. Thin bangles should usually be worn in pairs or groups, but before deciding on width or number, it is crucial to consider your body shape and bone structure.

Most fine bangles appear to be one solid piece but actually incorporate a hidden clasp into their design, enabling the wearer to slip it over the wrist with ease. This design is more popular among better jewelry because of its workmanship and quality.

Some people confuse a bangle with a cuff bracelet, but a cuff, while similar, fits closer to the wrist and usually incorporates a hinge mechanism.

The other major type of bracelet is known as the flexible bracelet. This type consists of a number of chain-like links or a series of motifs. Flexible bracelets are not as versatile as the bangle and in my opinion are best reserved for dressy occasions. An example of a flexible bracelet is the traditional charm bracelet. These have fallen out of vogue in recent years, but that doesn't necessarily mean they look out of synch with the fashions you choose. If you have a charm bracelet with sentimental value or if you just like the look, by all means wear it. Again let me stress: jewelry is a way of making you feel good about yourself, a way to express your personality. There are no rights and wrongs. If a charm bracelet personifies your style, it can only be right.

The same holds true for watches, which are almost always made in bracelet form. Though many people think of watches as functional items, they are jewelry too and can be wonderfully decorative — as well as keeping you on schedule! If you find a watch that expresses you, even though it is not the most fashionable style, that is the watch you should wear.

The typical everyday watch is a simple one with a leather band. It can be worn almost anywhere your normal daily routine takes you, but don't make the mistake of wearing it for participatory sports or special occasions. Such events require

Your everyday watch should be decorative but functional, whether the band is leather or metal.

their own timepieces. Your typical everyday watch probably cannot hold up to the rigors of most sports in which you take part. For equestrian sports, scuba diving, or even tennis, it's best to buy a sport watch that is shock and water proof.

The problem with wearing your leather-banded watch in the evening or to dressy affairs is that it looks badly out of place. Again, consider the rest of your ensemble. Would you wear espadrilles or penny loafers with your formal gown? Of course not. So why wear the same watch you wear with everyday clothes? A special occasion deserves a special watch, perhaps one encrusted with diamonds. If that's not financially feasible, a simple gold watch will do nicely.

But remember, if you don't have the right watch to wear to a gala event, it's better not to wear one at all. After all, you are there to enjoy yourself, to celebrate, and checking the time is, at the least, a trifle rude.

There is one piece of everyday jewelry which can and does go anywhere. I'm referring, of course, to the traditional wedding ring set. No matter how plain or fancy your wedding band, it is always acceptable to wear it.

In the United States, an engagement ring usually consists of a diamond solitaire, and the wedding band is a simpler version of the engagement ring. The two form a matching set and represent the only exception to the rule of not wearing more than one ring on a single finger. Because such rings are extremely personal, the style, cut, and metal are entirely a matter of personal preference. As with the purchase of any piece of jewelry, body shape and features must be considered. If the bridegroom wishes to surprise his fiancee, I advise shopping with her to get an idea of her likes and dislikes and also examining her hand type to determine what style will set it off to its best advantage.

And there are ways a woman can help her husband or bridegroom select jewelry right for her. For instance, one young

Special occasions deserve special watches such as these timepieces that will dress up any outfit.

woman who was looking forward to celebrating a wedding anniversary came into my salon recently. She happened to find a pair of earrings she adored. Knowing her husband would want to select something she would like, she asked me to call him and tell him her best friend had visited the salon, spied these earrings, and knew they were exactly right for his wife.

To some people such a scheme sounds devious, but I happen to think it's merely the sign of a smart woman who knows her husband would rather give her something she likes than waste his money on something wrong for her. I also find most men are grateful for suggestions — and usually follow them quickly.

Whether the ring is an engagement ring or not, no other piece of jewelry carries quite the same symbolism. Early rings were placed on the body as a means of preventing the soul from escaping. Today few people entertain such notions, nonetheless, a beautiful ring brings great joy to the soul and symbolizes mutual commitment.

Besides the wedding set, the major type of ring is called a cocktail or dinner ring. Such terms are really outdated, however, because they have come to mean any special-occasion ring. Such rings are not out of place unless, of course, they are too ostentatious for daytime wear.

Rings come in a variety of shapes and sizes, usually corresponding to the cut of the stone. Since rings fit closely to the finger and are most noticeable because people "talk" with their hands, everyone should take special care to select the style that is just right for their hand shape. Dome-shaped rings are especially popular now because they incorporate a setting that sits up high but is not overly large. Such a ring makes a strong statement without overwhelming, and most hands can wear a variation of the dome shape nicely.

Miscellaneous

The only remaining type of jewelry that you will encounter

on occasion is the pin. Not many women wear pins anymore, probably because they are no longer necessary for their original purpose, which was literally to hold clothes together. Also, pins are probably less popular because they are not exceptionally versatile. Most women buy pins for particular outfits instead of incorporating them into their entire wardrobe.

The right pin or brooch can work wonders for the right outfit, however, and for many people they represent a more whimsical method of expressing personal taste. Fashion designer Pauline Trigere, for instance, is known for wearing turtle pins, sometimes several at a time. Cosmetics queen Mary Kay Ash also likes to reward her associates with bumblebee pins.

Pins, particularly brooches such as these, have not been as popular recently, but they look lovely on the right woman.

Those women have selected from a classic type of pin — animal motifs. A diamond pin is also considered a timeless evening accessory. But generally, most women who wear pins today prefer more contemporary or art nouveau pieces. Again — and it is particularly important in this instance — you must consider how the pin relates to your overall body size and shape. The pin is a stationary object and must harmonize with its surroundings, including not only the outfit it is pinned to but the person in the outfit.

Regardless of the design, there are two basic pin styles, the brooch and the clip. A brooch is a stiff design mounted on a back that fastens with a pin, while a clip is a similar design employing a hinged back.

One of the most trendy pin looks to come along in recent years was the stickpin, a straight pin with an ornament on top and a guard on the bottom. The preppy look that prevailed in the first part of the '80s brought it back in style, but as quickly as that fashion trend came in, it went out. A stickpin looks dated with many of today's looser, more free flowing looks, but some women "stick" to it because it is most appropriate for their image. Lawyers, bankers, and other women who must

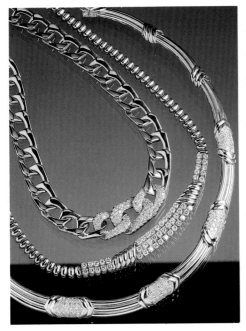

maintain a very conservative, businesslike appearance during the day are particularly fond of the stickpin because it enables them to dress up their usual business attire without appearing unprofessional.

I cite the stickpin as an example to repeat what I have tried to stress when discussing jewelry types: that there are no absolutes, no blanket rights and wrongs. Though certain jewelry styles are more popular today than others, that does not mean the style you select is unfashionable. If it's right for you, it's always in style.

To me, that's what style really is: not following the crowd so everyone is a clone of everyone else, but creating a statement through clothes and accessories that flatters your looks while expressing your feelings and attitudes. Those attitudes don't always have to be on the cutting edge of fashion — but they do have to be true to the person wearing them.

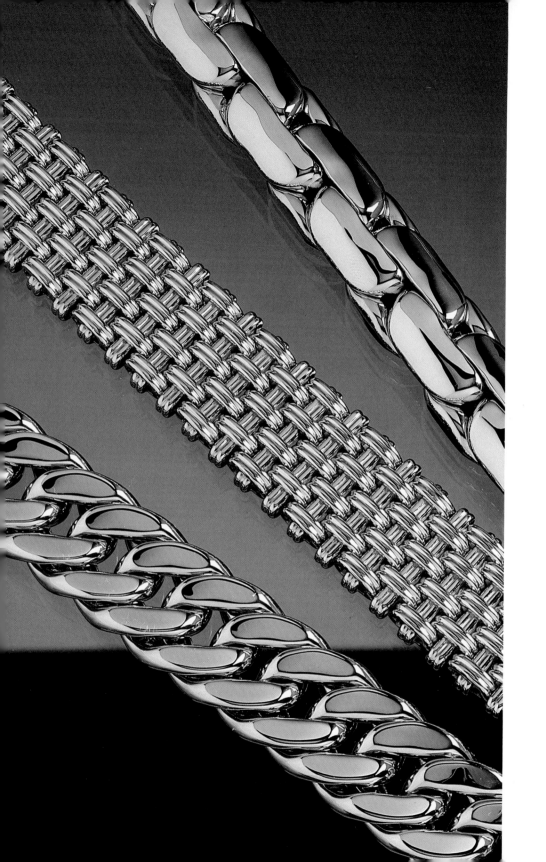

Chapter Two
Developing a Personal Sense of Jewelry Style

Through the centuries, various gemstones and metals have been worn for every purpose from matchmaking to warding off evil spirits and curing illness. Some people remain superstitious about such legends, but the main purpose of wearing jewelry has never changed: to enhance the beauty of the wearer. While the mystical powers of jewelry have proven to be myths, jewelry never fails — when properly selected — to add to the natural beauty of the wearer.

There is no one who cannot wear some type of jewelry and look good in it. The key is to find the type of jewelry that looks best on you. Just as certain wines go better with certain foods, certain jewelry pieces look better on some people than others.

Choosing jewelry, however, is more complicated. That's because there are several factors involved, including the size of the piece, the overall design, the metal in which it is set, and the color of the gems. These factors must be matched with your overall body size and shape, the size and shape of the body areas on which the jewelry will be worn; your skin tones, and your overall coloring, including hair and eye color.

Sound complicated? It is and it isn't. What it comes down to is learning to express yourself through an honest, candid assessment of your strengths and weaknesses. For some women this is next to impossible. I have known a few who insisted on wearing jewelry that simply did not look good on them. But most of the women I work with are eager to make the most of their purchases and are more than willing to take the time and effort to learn what is exactly right for them. With a little self analysis and knowledge of how to play up their assets and minimize any flaws, they have learned quickly what jewelry suits them best.

Have you ever wondered why the wonderful ring you bought never drew any compliments? Or why the necklace that looked so fabulous in the store looks all wrong at home? If you have, you undoubtedly would like to learn how to avoid such costly mistakes in the future. If you haven't, don't wait until you're disappointed in a purchase to take the time to learn the right approach.

The apparel and cosmetics industries long ago learned how to appeal to customers with the idea of informed buying. Many apparel stores and cosmetics companies employ consultants or knowledgeable salespeople to help customers who are unsure of what looks best on them, but jewelry has traditionally been left to impulse buying. That's especially ironic to me because fine jewelry usually represents a much more sizable monetary investment.

But there are many jewelers who are sadly lacking in this area. Most jewelers are excellent gemologists and infinitely learned about jewelry itself, but they are woefully deficient when it comes to keeping up with fashion and lifestyle trends. They may also be reluctant to advise a customer on what looks best with her figure and features, simply because they themselves are unsure. If a jeweler has a salon located in a store known for fashion, he is more likely to know what styles are "in" and what looks good on customers, merely because he works in that environment.

Even if the jeweler is knowledgeable about both gems and fashion, a smart shopper never relies solely on others for advice. No one knows your mind, body, and wardrobe the way you do, and once you've analyzed your needs and know what to look for, nothing is more fun than shopping for a wonderful piece of jewelry.

Body Proportions

The first and most important factor to consider is your overall body size. If your jewelry is out of synch with your size, you may create the wrong impression, even from a distance. I know some women who feel because they are large they cannot wear jewelry. They avoid it because they believe it calls attention to their bulk. So they go through life looking like Plain Jane, trying to blend into the wallpaper instead of playing up and emphasizing their strengths. And some small women sometimes make the same mistake for the opposite reason, saying they cannot wear jewelry because it overwhelms their size and features. Again, there are no women who cannot wear jewelry.

I am always amazed at the American preoccupation with size. There have been periods when large, ample figures have been greatly admired and periods when tiny figures were the rage. But except for excess weight, one cannot change what nature has bestowed in terms of bone structure and height. I wish that, instead of ignoring what they are or trying to make themselves into something they are not, more women would accept their bodies and make the most of them. It is merely a matter of finding your assets and building on those. Luckily, you are limited only by your imagination because there is such a diversity of colors and styles in jewelry pieces.

A general rule of thumb for body size is "small with small and big with tall." Size is often relative to those around you, but in most western societies, a woman is classified as **Petite,** if she is 5 feet 4 inches and under, **Average** if she is 5 feet 4 inches to 5 feet 7 inches, and **Tall** if she is over 5 feet 7 inches. But size is more than a matter of feet and inches. It also means bone structure. If you're small in stature but have large bones, you must take that into account when buying specific pieces such as necklaces and bracelets. The reverse holds true for large women who are small-boned.

The only way to determine your body size and shape is to take a good look in the mirror. But that look must be an honest one. Don't be overly hard on yourself, but just as you would not try to wear a size 4 dress if you have a size 12 body, you must not fool yourself. If you're taller or heavier than you'd like

Because of their narrow widths, bangles such as these look best when worn in pairs or groups.

32

Unless a tall woman is overly thin, her long neck is usually flattered by long earrings as shown here.

33

The color of many stones is associated with their place of origin. Most pigeon-blood colored rubies are from Burma, hence the term Burmese rubies, while darker, almost purplish brown stones are known as Siamese rubies because they come from Siam. Pale-pink rubies are often from Ceylon. The best sapphires, generally a cornflower blue, come primarily from Kashmir, while the most beautiful emeralds come from Colombia.

to be, admit it — but don't fret about it. Everyone has assets to build on, and usually there are many more assets than flaws. Once you have determined your body size and shape, keep these ideas in mind when making jewelry selections.

Petite: Thin, Average, Full-Figured

The **Petite** woman must take more care when selecting jewelry than any other. Because she is small, mistakes loom larger on her than on others. The proper choice, however, merely improves her appearance without anyone being consciously aware of the reason why.

Many small women for instance, have been connoisseurs of fine jewelry. The important thing is to identify and accept your size, to be proud of it because it is yours, instead of trying to appear to be something you are not. Even the best jewelry cannot make a small woman look 5 feet 10 inches tall. But it can make her look taller if that's what she wants, and most important, it can allow her to look her best.

Necklaces and bracelets are particularly important for the **Thin Petite** woman. She may have an overly delicate bone structure that tends to make her look thin, and because of their location, necklaces and bracelets tend to emphasize bones. The best choices are collar length necklaces, those which do not fit too tightly but rest against the neckbone, and may even help disguise the delicate bones, if necessary. Bangle bracelets are best because they don't emphasize the thinness of the wrist. Several narrow bangles are more flattering than wider types because they are more proportional to the thin petite woman's overall size. A prominent wrist bone is also played down with the help of a three dimensional, studded bracelet. Delicate bone structure is important to keep in mind when selecting a watch. In most cases, the best choice for the thin petite woman is a marquise or oval face that pulls the eye toward the hand and does not leave it lingering too long on an overly prominent wrist bone.

Bone structure is not a problem when it comes to selecting earrings, so the thin petite woman should concentrate on earrings that sweep up.

That's the best advice for the **Average Petite** woman as well. She should avoid drop or dangling earrings because they pull the viewer's eyes down instead of up. The small woman is not trying to appear tall, but neither does she wish to place undue emphasis on her size. For that reason she should select earrings that sweep up, angles that draw attention upward.

The proper necklace can also make or break the appearance of the average petite woman. A collar necklace is preferred because most small women of any body size have short necks; a tight choker cuts the line of the neck and is usually made of bulky materials that only emphasize the short space between chin and shoulder. Necklaces with v-shapes, those that draw the attention away from the face, are helpful. Longer necklaces that fall below the breast but above the waist, elongate the figure. The average petite woman should avoid cuff bracelets because their two-inch-plus widths look awkward on her figure.

The most important tip for the **Full-Figured Petite** is to avoid round shapes altogether, especially button or round earrings. Such shapes only emphasize roundness. Sharp geometric shapes provide greater contrast, more lines and angles to attract the viewer.

Also, even though she is short in inches, and because she is full-figured, the full figured petite should avoid tiny jewelry. It's best to select a medium size, whether that be a necklace, bracelet, watch, or any other piece. When buying necklaces and bracelets it's a good idea for the full-figured petite to avoid pieces that fit closely to the skin. A bangle bracelet is preferable to a cuff; a collar necklace looks better than a choker. Again, the trick is to accent your strengths and downplay your weaknesses.

Average: Thin, Average, Full-Figured

The woman of **Average** height has a wider range of jewelry choices than her smaller counterpart — because her height is neither a benefit or a disadvantage, she doesn't have to concern herself with minimizing or maximizing it. She can instead choose from a wide variety of pieces. Earring choices are virtually unlimited, depending on facial and lobe shape, of course; but the average woman is usually wise to select geometric shapes such as triangles, squares, and ovals because they create added excitement. The average woman should also wear wide bracelets rather than narrow ones, particularly if she is **Thin Average.** Medium-sized bracelets are more proportional to the average woman's size than thinner ones.

Similarly, the average woman can wear necklaces of any length unless she is **Full-Figured Average.** In that case, she should be especially careful not to draw attention to the breast area, avoiding necklaces which rest on the breastline, and making sure not to wear too many necklaces which also tends to emphasize the chest area. She should also be certain to wear jewelry of medium size, not a delicate piece, because it will look out of proportion if it is too small.

Tall: Thin, Average, Full-Figured

The woman with the widest range of choices of all is the tall woman. Ever wonder why most top models are tall? Because they are the most versatile when it comes to wearing clothes and accessories. A lanky lady can carry off looks that would overwhelm other women. Unfortunately, except for those top models, a lot of women are still uncomfortable with being tall. If you are above average in height, I urge you to appreciate it. When it comes to wearing jewelry, your choices are wide. But just as the right jewelry won't add inches to a small woman, it won't subtract them from the tall woman. If you accept what the yardstick tells you, you won't want to do that anyway. Instead, concentrate on selecting the pieces that complement your height.

The **Thin Tall** woman may wish to de-emphasize her height because it tends to accentuate her thinness. In that case, the most important trick to keep in mind is to wear choker necklaces, which cut the line of the neck and coincidentally de-emphasize height. Necklaces made of stones or pearls of the same size, instead of graduated pieces, work best for this effect.

The **Average Tall** woman has plenty of space between her earlobe and shoulder, so she can wear any earring except tiny buttons, which will look lost. Long pendants and dangling earrings are especially flattering to tall women.

Similarly, because her neck is often long and there is a long area between neck and waist, the tall woman can also wear almost any length necklace, depending on personal preference. She also has a wide range of bracelet choices — as long as she stays away from delicate pieces which tend to look awkward.

This is particularly true for the **Full-Figured Tall** woman. If you like thin bracelets but have a full body shape, wear several thin bracelets together to give a heavier overall feeling, or a couple of thick bracelets. When choosing necklaces, the full-figured tall woman should avoid oversized beads. While they may make the neck look shorter in some instances, they can also make it look fuller, which is not the best choice. Necklaces should be loose and tapering and of medium size.

Facial Shape

After considering your body size and shape, it's time to analyze your **Facial Shape.**

There are four basic facial shapes: the round, oval, square, and heart-shaped. Each of them requires a little thought before buying jewelry, because you don't want to overemphasize your facial shape, but you do want to complement it.

Beware of colored diamonds billed as "treated." Such stones are poor-quality diamonds that have been bombarded atomically to change their hue. Treated diamonds are not highly regarded.

Any shape which emphasizes vertical lines is flattering to the woman with a broad face.

Round shapes tend to broaden a round face.

39

If you have a **Round** face, don't accent it by wearing round earrings, no matter how big or small. Stick with triangles, wings, or ovals that fit close to the face without following the line of the ear too closely. You want to create interest in this area, but not enough to pull the viewers' eyes along the contour of your face. The best way to complement a round face is by contrasting the basic shape with other shapes, particularly those with lots of interesting angles. Loops are perfectly acceptable for the round face because they draw the attention down instead of around, but they're even better when combined with a small geometric shape attached to the lobe. This style doesn't widen the ear and thus lengthens the face.

The woman with an **Oval** face can wear round shapes, button, or loop earrings easily, but she looks especially attractive in triangular shapes. The oval faced woman must be careful, however, to stay away from very tiny earrings. Her shape looks much better with a slightly larger size because larger earrings help fill out the shadows from high cheekbones.

Dangling earrings look good next to an oval face if they are not too long. The oval face can often be a thin face, and earrings that are round at the base and taper upward, around the rim of the ear, minimize that problem effectively.

The oval face may also feature a long nose. That can be downplayed by avoiding earrings that follow the line of the ear or have wings that sweep up. Vertical lines only emphasize these areas, which is why the oval faced woman usually looks best in round or triangle shapes.

The **Square-Faced** woman also has several factors to keep in mind. This facial type usually needs a little softening, not accenting, and the most effective way to do that is through the use of marquise or oval-shaped earrings. These shapes draw the attention up or down, not sideways. Round earrings are a poor choice because they provide too great a contrast and look awkward. Long or dangling earrings are acceptable as long as they are not too thick. The woman with a square face should emphasize length instead of width.

On the other hand, the **Heart-Shaped** face needs those round shapes. The focal point of this facial shape tends to be the chin, so the best way to complement the heart shaped face is through round shapes which balance against the pointedness of the lower half of the face. For this facial shape, long, narrow earrings should be avoided, and rounder, wider shapes are preferred.

There is one other factor to take into consideration when analyzing your facial shape. That factor is your hair length. Fortunately, most hair stylists today adapt hair length to facial shapes, so what fits one generally fits the other.

Keep in mind, however, that short hair is generally accepted best with button earrings. These complement the style but don't exaggerate it. Chin-length hair can carry any style earring, especially dangling or larger button types. Long hair, that which falls past the shoulders, usually requires an equally dramatic jewelry style. Dangling or pendant earrings show up better, while smaller pieces tend to be overlooked easily. The best example of the dramatic jewelry that goes with long hair is that worn by entertainer Cher, when her hair fell past her waist, or singer Crystal Gale, whose knee-length hair would look ridiculous with a tiny stud for an earring.

Many women may see the areas I've discussed so far as obvious factors to consider when buying jewelry. I hope so. But in my work, I've noticed that few women ever take into account another crucial area, the earlobe. Many women buy this all-important type of jewelry without giving a thought to the shape of the body area it will fit most closely. But earlobes vary widely in shape, and since earrings fit closely and emphasize this area, it's vital that it be considered.

A **Long Ear Lobe,** for instance, requires a button earring that will cover the lobe and soften the length. Don't buy loop

Large earrings such as these with cushion shape complement the oval face.

The square-faced woman should emphasize length instead of width. These earrings are an excellent choice because they draw the eye upwards and not across.

earrings because they emphasize the length of the lobe. It's best to cover a long lobe as it is a feature that looks best when minimized.

Should you have an occasion or outfit that calls for a dangling earring, however, choose one that has a round shape at the top. And in almost all cases, large earrings are a good choice because they disguise the lobe size.

Average Lobes can handle almost any type earring because they are not extreme enough to warrant undue attention. Proportional sizes are most complementary, but large buttons are usually too overwhelming.

A special word to the woman who has a small lobe or one that is attached directly to the head, which gives the effect of no lobe at all. This type lobe is best covered because there is not enough there to work with, and any dangling or loop type earring will appear to be attached too close to the bone. Any shape which follows the direction of the ear, covering the lobe and drawing attention upward, is most appropriate.

Hand Shape

One final area to take into account when buying jewelry is the hand. This is a body area that attracts a great deal of attention because people "talk" with their hands. Because the hands are constantly moving, it's like waving a flag in front of someone. And when people respond to that flag, it's best to have a ring that flatters your hand instead of one that detracts.

The biggest factor when buying a ring is the setting. And what usually determines the setting is the cut of the main stone. There are several basic cuts that are applied primarily to diamonds but also to other stones. The most popular shape is the round or brilliant cut. It is used most often and is the most popular because it usually shows a diamond's fire more than any other cut. Other basic cuts include the pear (pointed at one end, rounded at the other, like the fruit); the marquise (pointed at both ends and named after the mistress of Louis XIV); the oval (elongated, but rounded at both ends); the emerald (rectangular with faceted corners, so named because it sets off its namesake stone especially well); the square; the cushion (square with rounded corners); and the heart-shaped.

The length of the fingers is the determining factor when purchasing rings. Women with **Long Fingers,** like tall women, can handle almost any style. They should however, avoid extremely oversized rings which can often look exaggerated. When it comes right down to it, no one can really carry off an "oversized" ring. A ring must be in proportion to your hand, but what is big for one hand might be just right for another. Strive for appropriate, not theatrical looks. If the long-fingered hand is also overly thin, oval or round settings are best. These shapes soften the look and flatter a somewhat thin, but elegant hand.

The hand with **Short Fingers** should be adorned only with settings that remain within the knuckle. The setting or stone that extends past the knuckle only accentuates the hand's shortness and makes it look less elegant. Oval or marquise shapes elongate the hand and make good choices for short fingers. Round solitaire settings are acceptable because of their simplicity, but large round settings should be avoided. If a large ring is what you really want, however, opt for a dome shape or a high setting that won't overpower the short hand.

When buying a ring, it is most important to keep comfort in mind. The hand is a working, functioning body area, as opposed to the earlobe, which doesn't put forth any effort. Don't forsake comfort for looks. Measure the length of your knuckle and buy only what allows you to move your finger freely. Besides, if a ring is uncomfortable it's probably too big for your hand anyway.

By now, after analyzing your overall body shape and individual areas, you are probably wondering how to assimilate

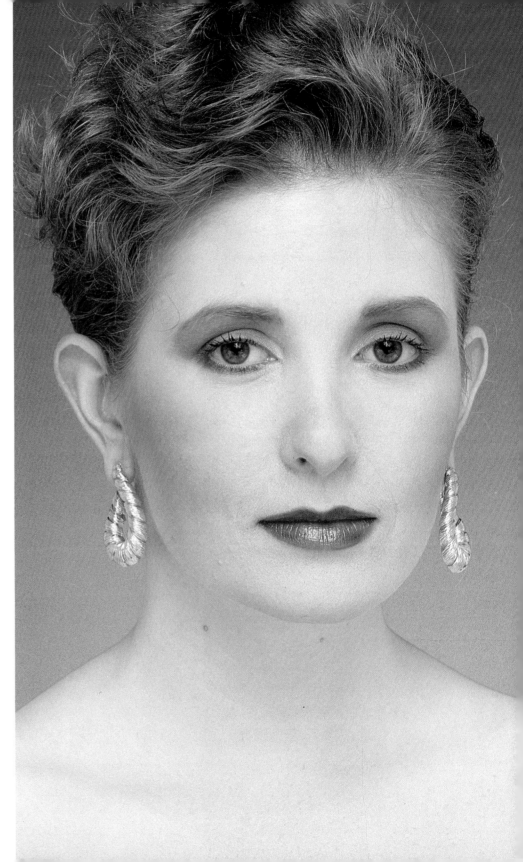

Long dangling earrings only accentuate long ear lobes. A better choice is a round ear clip.

The very small or attached ear lobe is the only type that really requires a pierced earring. If the woman is petite, a small earring is appropriate; otherwise she may choose a larger one to cover the indefinite ear lobe.

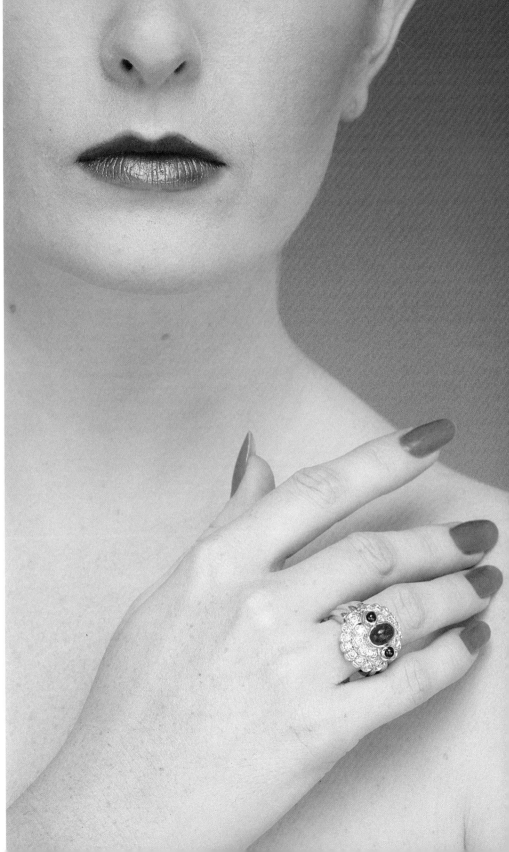

Long fingers are flattered by round settings which minimize the length of the fingers.

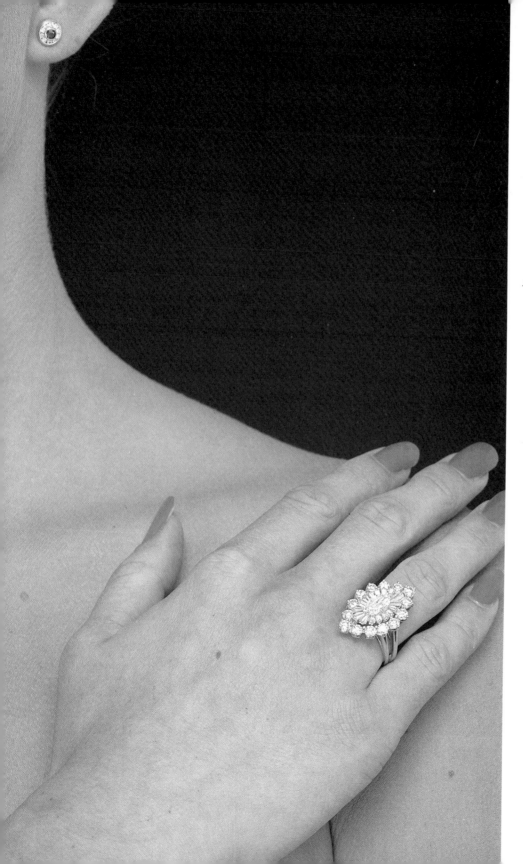

*Oval or marquise settings flatter the
short-fingered hand.*

and use all this information. It's not as complicated as it sounds. It's entirely possible you are a tall, thin woman with a round face, long ear lobes, and short fingers. Or a petite, average woman with a square face, attached lobes and average fingers. Go back to basics. Analyze which of your features stands out the most, and what type of jewelry (Chapter One) you prefer for your lifestyle.

You may, for instance, dislike wearing earrings altogether. In that case, the shape of your earlobe is not an important area to consider. But if you love rings, by all means, take your hands into consideration. Or your body shape may stand out before your facial shape or neck length. Generally however, many of these characteristics go together. It's best to analyze yourself, your lifestyle, and the image you project, as an interrelated whole. As you do that, your best features will undoubtedly come to the forefront and the flaws that seem so large will begin to fade in importance. Don't forget, that's what jewelry is all about: enhancing one's own personal sense of beauty.

The reason for devoting this time and effort to self-analysis is to develop self-confidence through preparation. Once you know what is right for you, you begin to develop a lifelong sense of your own style, which is far more effective than having one imposed on you. There's a world of difference between being a fashion victor and a fashion victim.

There are no absolute rights and wrongs — and there are even more factors to take into consideration after you complete the first analysis.

I'm talking about color, of course — your coloring, the color of the clothes you wear, and the color of the gems you buy. All this may seem like a lot of work, but considering the relatively large amount of money you'll spend on jewelry over a lifetime, isn't it better to buy wisely, knowing your purchase will stand the test of time, than to buy on impulse and regret it later?

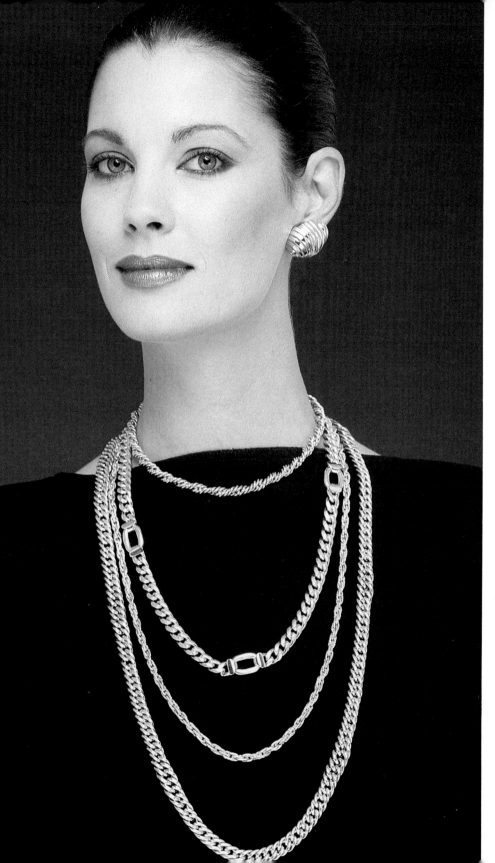

Choose the necklace length that is right for you, from the collar length necklace to one of the longer styles.

51

Chapter Three
Color—Yours and Your Jewelry

In recent years there has been more and more talk about color. Colors that flatter, colors that detract. Colors that lift, colors that subdue.

At first such talk was dismissed as having little practical value, but with time we've realized there is a great deal to be said for examining the colors that make us feel good about ourselves and others.

Who does not enjoy the awesome hues of a rainbow after a storm? Or the glorious colors of spring? Think of the bright turquoise-blue sky, the emerald-green grass and the deep sapphire blue of cornflowers. What I love about my business is that those same beautiful colors are immortalized in gems. The beauty of owning fine jewelry is the sense of being able to hold a piece of that sky, or viewing that green grass all year round, of wearing a cornflower any season, not just mentally but literally.

But not everyone likes the same things. Some people prefer violets to cornflowers, for instance. That's why everyone contemplating a jewelry purchase should take time to think about not only what they like but what colors look good on them. One of the main reasons to accessorize clothing with jewelry is to add a spot of color.

It makes no sense to leave jewelry out when analyzing your color needs. As I have said before, gems represent a much more sizable investment than clothing, so it makes dollar sense as well as aesthetic sense to devote a little thought to what materials look best on you and your clothes.

In the last few years, color analyst Carole Jackson has attracted a great deal of attention with her theory that natural beauty is discovered through matching clothing colors to skin and hair tones. In my opinion, *Color Me Beautiful* is one of the best things to come along on the American clothing and beauty scene in years. I say this because the book gives women practical advice on how to make the most of their assets, and gives them confidence to shop wisely. Such advice has been sorely needed, and although I am a jeweler, not a color analyst, it's become obvious to me that color analysis is an idea whose time has come and one that is destined to become ingrained in the American way of shopping.

Through the years, without consciously trying, I have noticed that some stones flatter certain women and some don't. It takes a little time to learn all the stones from nature's fabulous spectrum, but it's easy to identify your own hair color, skin tone, and clothing colors. When it comes to the jewelry itself, there are two basic areas of color: the metal of which the jewelry is made, and the gems or other materials which are set into that metal.

While there are only three basic metals to be concerned with when buying jewelry, gems are not so easily classified.

It used to be fashionable to refer to the "Big Four" — diamonds, emeralds, rubies, and sapphires — as "precious," primarily because of their beauty, scarcity, and price. Other colored stones have been labeled "semiprecious," but it is an unfortunate term. Though the Big Four are still more expensive on the average than other colored stones, a fine example of a "semiprecious" stone can cost more than a poor example of a "precious" gem. The term is obviously more than a little misleading. Therefore, I recommend dismissing the terms "precious" and "semiprecious" from your jewelry vocabulary altogether.

Metals

The three basic metals are identified primarily by color. Silver, of course, is known for its shiny "silver" hue; gold is best known for its bright yellow color; and platinum is a whitish metal that resembles silver. What many people do not realize is that gold actually comes in different colors from white to pink, depending on which alloy is added.

Fine gold, that which is 99.9 percent pure, is called 24-karat

An example of fine colored stones, this pastel multi-color ensemble would look best on a blonde or brunette, but it's not a strong choice for a redhead because she needs more vibrant colors.

gold. Though it is a beautiful bright yellow color, 24-karat gold is too soft to work with, and too soft to hold up under regular use, making it inappropriate for jewelry. Most fine jewelers use 18-karat gold, which consists of 75 percent gold and 25 percent alloy. White gold may have the same amount of gold, but the alloy used to strengthen it gives it a silvery or steel-gray color. If you prefer a metal of this shade, I recommend platinum.

Platinum is a silvery-looking metal that is also soft yet is durable. It is more expensive than gold but not as popular simply because its color is not as versatile or appealing. Silver is considerably cheaper than either gold or platinum, and while it is wonderful for casual, fun jewelry, few pieces of fine jewelry are made from it. That's partially because silver is an extremely soft metal which does not hold up under constant use, but more important it has simply never caught the imagination of fine jewelers and customers. Silver is imminently suitable for Indian style jewelry and sets off turquoise well, but for the most part, its color does not set off stones as effectively as other metals. Generally yellow gold is the most flattering metal for both stones and people.

18-karat yellow gold and platinum.

As a lover of fine gems, it's natural that I prefer jewelry with both metals and stones. But there are many stunning pieces of jewelry crafted from metals alone, particularly necklaces and earrings. Plain metal pieces are particularly appropriate for daytime wear or to accent casual sportswear. But there are also numerous lovely finishes which dress up plain metal and make them just the right accent for evening as well. When analyzing your coloring and self-image, take into consideration whether you prefer the simplicity of metals alone or the more opulent look of gems. Everyone needs a little of each, but it's good to know where your preference lies.

Gems

Most people find gems as entrancing as I do, and find the

combination of metals and beautifully colored gems irresistable. The best-known stones — diamonds, emeralds, rubies, and sapphires — are the most expensive and not coincidentally the most brilliantly colored. There are many other gems, but these four have been valued above the rest for thousands of years.

Ironically, the most highly prized stone of all is actually colorless. I am referring, of course, to the classic diamond. Diamonds have captured the fancy of men and women because of their clarity or lack of color. This very feature, however, gives the stone an ability to refract and disperse light, letting loose many sparkling rainbows within the stone that are unmatched by any other gem.

Not all diamonds are colorless, however. There are colored diamonds, referred to as "fancies," which come in natural shades of blue, pink, brown, yellow, green, and rarest of all — red. Though the term "fancies" is widely used, I dislike it. Just as "precious" and "semiprecious" are misleading, "fancies" to me denotes something which has been hyped up unnecessarily. The beauty of a natural colored diamond speaks volumes for itself and needs no such term to describe it. It is not a term familiar to the average customer because so few people are aware diamonds come in colors. Beware, however, of stones which are artificially treated; they are not highly valued.

Natural colored diamonds may be even more expensive than the traditional clear diamond. In fact, one of history's most famous diamonds, the Hope Diamond, is blue.

Though diamonds are generally the most prized stone, rubies are actually rarer and often cost more. Rubies and sapphires both come from the same mineral family, corundum. All corundum that is not colored red is referred to as sapphire. Rubies vary in color from pale pink to crimson, but the most highly valued shade is the color of pigeon blood, a full rich shade with a hint of orange. A bluish or black tint makes the ruby less valuable.

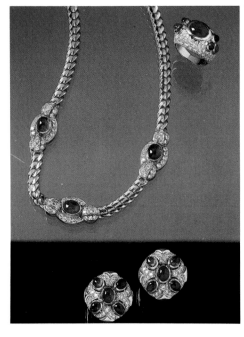

The Big Four: rubies, emeralds, and sapphires cut en cabochon, surrounded by tiny faceted diamonds.

Sapphires differ from rubies only in their color. The best-known shade is blue, but sapphires also come in shades of yellow, orange, green, violet, and pink. Blue sapphires are the most highly sought after, particularly if the shade is a deep cornflower color.

Both rubies and sapphires are also sometimes marked by another color: white. Some rubies and sapphires are more translucent, almost milky, and contain long parallel crystals forming the appearance of a star. This effect is called "asterism" or "star rubies" or "star sapphires."

Despite the lure of diamonds, rubies, and sapphires, some people feel there is no jewel like the emerald. This striking, bright green stone, a member of the beryl mineral family, is also more rare than diamonds. Light green stones are called beryl, but medium-light to medium-dark stones are known as emeralds.

While color, cut, clarity, and weight all figure heavily into the value of a diamond, color is the most important factor when it comes to emeralds. Unlike diamonds, emeralds are almost never without flaws, so the deeper the green of an emerald, the more valuable it is.

While those stones comprise the Big Four, there is another jewelry material, equally prized, and known for a remarkable color spectrum: pearls. Unlike the Big Four stones, pearls are opaque with colors ranging from golden to pink and even black. The classic pearl is a creamy white hue with a slight hint of pink. Pearls, while lacking the fire of many gems, have a strong lustre or ability to reflect light. There are two basic types of pearls: sea pearls and freshwater or baroque. Both come in several colors, but the distinguishing factors are their shapes. Sea pearls are usually round, while freshwater pearls are small and irregularly shaped. Whether freshwater or sea pearls, natural colors are always preferred over dyed or tinted varieties, which are not considered fine jewelry.

Freshwater pearls (left) are small and irregularly shaped, while sea pearls (center and right) are usually round. Note the various casts — hints of yellow and pink and blue.

When it comes to selecting gifts, I feel there is no substitute for pearls. They are always appropriate, for any person at any time, because they are so incredibly versatile. And because they are such precious gifts from nature, pearls are wonderfully romantic.

The gems I have discussed thus far are the best known, but there are numerous other fine colored stones and materials. They are usually less expensive but nonetheless are most attractive and well worth collecting. What I like best about these other stones is that they offer more subtle colors that complement the primary hues of the Big Four. Since we are discussing gems on the basis of color, let me touch on a few of the more popular and versatile stones by color families.

Pearls are considered extremely versatile because of their neutrality, but there are several other materials in shades of white, including coral, ivory, and opals. Like pearls, coral is not a stone but a gift from the sea. These animal skeletons come in several colors, from oxblood to white. Darker colored coral is generally more costly because divers must go deeper to retrieve it, but I like white coral not only because it is affordable but also because it is a suitable alternative to ivory.

Many people prize ivory, which comes from elephant tusks, but I never recommend it. To me, one of the most fascinating aspects of collecting fine jewels is their source: nature. And nothing shows less gratitude for those gifts than the senseless slaughter of magnificent animals. Jewels are wonderful luxuries, items of adornment, not something on which one's survival depends, such as food or clothing.

Buying ivory makes even less sense to me because it is not a wise jewelry purchase. It does not hold its color well, yellowing through the years, losing the striking whiteness people desire. Coral is a wonderful alternative. Another white stone to consider is the opal. Opals are beautiful, with their fiery rainbows, and also come in black, clear, and red.

Black onyx, well deserving its increased popularity, is especially striking when paired with yellow gold or diamonds.

Unlike the white color family, there are few black stones to choose from. Black onyx is the most familiar, and luckily it is a relatively inexpensive material. It has become more and more popular in recent years because fashion designers have become enamored with black. Black onyx almost always needs to be paired with another stone, preferably diamonds or lots of yellow gold, for best effect.

Blue stones have also been increasingly popular in recent years, and luckily there are numerous alternatives to the more expensive sapphires. The most popular is probably aquamarine, which is named for the sea water it resembles. Colors range from light to deep blue with darker stones most valued. Another dark-blue stone that has been popular through the ages is lapis lazuli. This stone comes in a royal blue and is flecked with gold pyrite, giving it a versatility that allows it to fit into almost any color scheme.

Still another blue stone is tanzanite, which is a bluish violet hue. Perhaps the most markedly different blue stone, however, is the turquoise. Turquoise is an opaque sky-blue color that is traditionally associated with Indian-style jewelry. It is gaining favor as a contemporary material, however, but there is one drawback to turquoise: like ivory, it changes color as it ages, acquiring a yellow tinge that can spoil its beauty.

In the purple color family, there are two choices, amethysts and kunzite. Amethysts are one of my favorite fashion stones because they are relatively inexpensive and have a marvelous deep-purple color. Kunzite is paler, coming in violet or pink.

Ironically, one of the largest color families in gems is also one least utilized by fashion designers: green. Green is not included in a lot of designer collections because many people look sallow in it, but there are many green gemstones to choose from for accents, including cat's eye, jade, malachite, and peridot. Cat's eye is a milky gem that ranges in color from

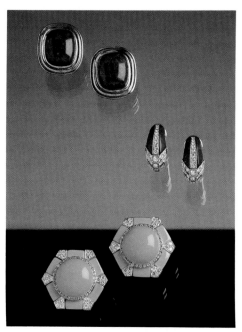

Two stones that captured the imaginations of ancient craftsmen shown here in their contemporary settings. Note the flecks of gold pyrite within the lapis lazuli (top and center) and the sky-blue color that turquoise exhibits at the height of its power.

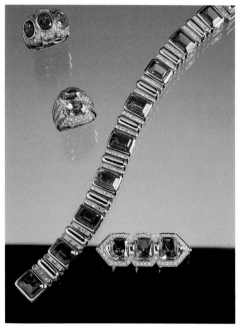

A veritable rainbow, tourmalines present a less costly option to those who love color.

Amethysts make it easy to see why purple was so often the preferred color of royalty.

honey yellow to green, with a bamboo green shade being the most desirable. When properly cut, cat's eye has a brilliant whitish line down the center, giving it the appearance of a feline eye.

Jade is traditionally associated with a rich green color but also comes in lavender, orange, pink, white, and black. The traditional green, known as Imperial jade, is the most expensive but does not translate well to contemporary looks. A more handsome stone, in my opinion, is malachite, a banded green gem with beautiful color. And for the person desiring a pale green, there is always the peridot. Peridot is not particularly popular, but for someone looking for a pale lime-green stone, it is a perfect choice.

Two of the most popular and versatile stones are gems that come in a variety of colors. I'm referring, of course, to tourmaline and topaz. Tourmalines are a popular and inexpensive stone that come in a rainbow, from yellow to pink, green, and blue. Pink is the hottest color today because of the recent trend to bright hues, but blue is also coming on strong, particularly as an alternative to the more expensive aquamarine. The pale red tourmaline is known as rubellite and is a costly stone. Like tourmalines, topazes also come in many colors, including yellow, orange, pink, and blue.

One of my favorite stones is not one color but two colors at once! Alexandrite is a most unusual stone: by day it is a mossy dark green; by night it is a raspberry red. It is an expensive stone, but if you can only afford one gem yet still crave a change every now and then, alexandrite is hard to beat.

Hair

Now that you're familiar with what colors you have to choose from in gems, it's time to match those with your own coloring. The largest area of color to be concerned with is obviously your hair. Even though the top of the head is often farthest away from certain pieces of jewelry, it is nonetheless the body area that speaks of color first. And your natural hair color generally dictates your skin tones as well.

The woman who has the most choice when it comes to accenting hair color is the **Blonde.** Her hair is usually light enough to be considered almost neutral. But what looks best on the blonde are dark stones because they provide a more striking contrast than pastels. Black onyx, black opals, emeralds, rubellite, and sapphires are good choices because brighter stones stand out best against a neutral background. Pearls with a creamy or pink cast are also effective.

Bright stones are also best for the **Redhead.** Greens and blues are her most flattering colors, including emeralds, and sapphires. The redhead can also wear amethysts well but should avoid rubies because the deep red usually clashes with most red hair tones. Redheads should also avoid any rust-colored, brown, yellow, or salmon-colored stone, because they too fail to blend well. Pink tourmalines make poor choices because they clash, but the more subtle pink hue of pearls is quite flattering.

For the woman with **Brown** hair, pastels are the most attractive stones. Tourmalines, aquamarines, and corals are excellent selections, and jade also looks most becoming. Deep, dark stones, such as black onyx and black opals should be avoided because they do not provide enough contrast to attract attention.

The **Dark Brunette** looks best in greens, reds, pastels, and golden colors. These shades provide the most contrast while deep blues and blacks do not. To wear dark stones, a dark-haired woman must surround them with a lighter, contrasting stone, preferably diamonds.

Forget all the rules about contrast if you have **Gray, Silver,** or **White** hair. Dark stones such as sapphires, emeralds, and rubies are terrific, but diamonds are impossible to beat. For some reason the sparkle of diamonds only increases when set

In years past, these rings might have been referred to as "cocktail" or "dinner" rings. Today they can go from day into evening, as long as they are worn appropriately. Shown here, the popular (blue) aquamarine and the lesser known (purple) kunzite.

Redheads look best in dark stones which contrast their pale skin and striking hair.

*Redheads wear vibrant colors
beautifully but pastel stones such as these tend
to look washed out.*

Pastels are fabulous on women with brown or dark hair.

Blondes have endless freedom when it comes to choosing color, but darker stones, such as these emeralds, are particularly striking.

off by similarly colored hair.

Diamonds are best mounted in gold rather than platinum, however, as you can have too much of a good thing. Black is also stunning for the woman with silver hair.

Skin

The second most important area of personal color is the skin. This factor is less obvious than hair coloring but does make a difference and should be considered. Black women should be especially careful to avoid dark stones because they provide little contrast unless paired with diamonds. Opt for lighter stones in pastel shades. Platinum is also a more suitable metal for black women than gold because it provides a softer, more subtle contrast.

Skin tones are especially important when selecting pearls. Generally you should try to match the cast of the pearl with the shade of your skin. The pearl should blend with, not fight, your complexion. That's why redheads are often wise to select pearls with a pink cast; blondes should opt for a creamy cast; and dark-haired women should select a pure white pearl.

The only bit of body color which is not of major importance when selecting jewelry is the eye. This spot of color is located so far away from most jewelry pieces and is so small that it does not affect jewelry selection for the most part. If you do have truly striking eyes, of course, you should make the most of them by matching them with a stunning stone. A former beauty queen came into my salon one day and when I saw her deep-blue eyes, I knew nothing would look as wonderful on her as blue sapphires. We tried them and her eyes set the stones off beautifully — and vice versa.

What is far more important is to take into account the color of the clothes you'll be wearing. Any item of clothing is large enough to call attention to itself, so the jewelry must not only blend but blend beautifully for full effect.

Unlike other stones, diamonds are composed of one single element: carbon. Common pencil lead and diamonds are made of the same material; their atoms are merely arranged differently.

Most people rarely wear solid colors all the time, but every outfit has one color that dominates the others. When trying to select appropriate jewelry, it's most important to take that color into account. For instance, rubies may set your skin and hair color off beautifully, but if you've decided to wear pink, the stone may look ill-chosen. Gems do not have to match the clothes you're wearing, but they should provide a suitable contrast or blend compatibly.

Some color combinations go together naturally, but if you're unsure what to pair with what, make certain you're showing good taste by following a few basic guidelines.

When it comes to wearing **Red,** any blue, white, gold, black, or green stone blends nicely. Red stones are also appropriate in any shade, from cherry to scarlet. It's best, however to avoid pinks, yellows, and purples.

Safe stones to pair with **Blue** include red, other blues, black, white, and gold. There are few stones that don't go well with blue, but these are the most attractive.

I happen to know of one woman who wears **Yellow** every day, but not many women show it off that well. Black is the most striking color to wear with yellow because of the marked contrast. Pearls with a golden cast are also wonderful, and blues and greens go nicely. Yellow stones should be worn only if they match perfectly — an off shade appears sickly. Similarly, it's best to avoid chalky-white pearls because they look washed out. Reds and oranges also do not flatter a yellow outfit.

On the other hand, almost everyone and everything goes well with **White.** As a neutral color, both pale and dark stones set it off nicely. Pastels are wonderfully appropriate for a crisp spring look, while dark stones go nicely with a winter white or ivory. Only yellow stones should be avoided because they fail to stand out.

Like white, **Black** is a neutral color that can carry almost any stone. The only absolute negatives are deep sapphires,

The already stunning combination of rubies and diamonds is dramatically enhanced when set off against blue.

which do not show well, and black onyx, unless it is highlighted with lots of gold or contrasting stones. A black dress with plain black onyx earrings or other black onyx jewelry looks plain instead of understated. The same black dress with a black onyx and diamond earring is smashing.

As I mentioned previously, few clothing designers employ **Green** these days as most women do not wear it well. If you can wear green, select deep stones in shades of red, purple, black, and blue. Pearls of any cast except gray also go nicely, as do paler stones such as salmon, coral, and yellow. Green stones generally do not work, however, as it's difficult to match the colors exactly.

Pink clothes look especially good with pastel stones. Pearls are particularly attractive, as are dark stones such as black. Only reds clash badly with pink.

When wearing **Gray,** jewelry is difficult to choose. Black is very appealing with gray, and so is red. Pearls make an excellent choice, but pastels look good only with light gray. Stay away from dark-blue and green stones.

There aren't many women who wear **Orange** on a regular basis, which is good because, like gray, it is a difficult color to accessorize. Red, black, green, and other oranges are acceptable, as are some pastels. Avoid pink, purple, and yellow.

Purple is one of those colors that can be paired with many stones. Purple looks good with dark colors such as black and green and most pastels are also pretty with it. Pink, however, tends to look washed out next to purple. Avoid blue shades because there is too much similarity in color, and oranges because they can clash badly.

By now, you're undoubtedly wondering how you'll ever keep straight what gem colors to wear with what clothing colors, what jewels to wear to best set off your hair and skin, and so forth. Let me reassure you that after a while such knowledge becomes second nature. It's simply a matter of

At one time widows wore rings on their thumbs to indicate their marital status.

taking stock of your most outstanding features and deciding how to play them up to your advantage. While it sounds hopelessly complex, you'll also find in most cases that your hair, skin, clothing, and jewelry become a package deal. After a little personal analysis you'll discover quickly what is best for you, and learn to discard what doesn't flatter you.

And it is worth the effort. One of my best customers is a redhead with pink skin. When she first came to me 15 years ago, she expressed a fondness for pink and yellow stones. But those colors were not the best for her, and she changed to the more vibrant blue, black, and white, which has made a dramatic difference in her look. She's been pleased enough by it to keep coming back all these years!

Remember that since jewelry is a lasting investment in beauty, these are items you'll be wearing for years to come. It took the forces of nature centuries to form one wonderful gem — the least you can do is take a few minutes to decide which of those gems you want to wear for a lifetime.

Chapter Four
Designer Do's and Don'ts

Clothes make the man (or woman). This has probably been a popular axiom ever since clothes first gained importance as a fashion item rather than simply a protection against the elements. Though everyone agrees that one's personality means more than any skirt and blouse, it's also true that what we wear is a palpable expression of that personality. Clothing has been elevated in recent years to an art form, a method of expressing personality in a way that adds a bit of individuality in an increasingly mass-produced world.

But while clothing is an important element, it does not stand alone, any more than an entree makes a meal. To present a complete image, one must not only dress appropriately but also find the most flattering makeup, hair style, and accessories.

Many women appreciate beautiful clothes but unfortunately do not know how to put that total image together. They buy wonderful, quality apparel with impressive designer labels but then pair it with the wrong handbag or earrings. Such clothes cost tens of thousands of dollars, and unfortunately, the effort and money are wasted when accessorized incorrectly.

Certain designers have developed reputations for signature looks and can be easily recognized. A true fashion fan, for instance, can tell immediately that numerous tiny pleats are the mark of Mary McFadden; that Albert Nipon employs lots of feminine detailing, especially buttons and bows; and that Zandra Rhodes is synonymous with outlandish avant-garde looks.

Even the person who professes not to follow fashion knows more than she realizes. Did you ever watch Cher cavort across the television screen? If so, you're familiar with the glamorous, eye-popping costumes that shout the name of Bob Mackie. And if you've ever seen photographs of First Lady Nancy Reagan attending a luncheon engagement, you've probably spied a timeless, tasteful Adolfo suit.

It's surprising, however, the number of women who buy such clothes regularly but fail to take the overall feeling into account when compiling a jewelry wardrobe. They wear a dress they like and a piece of jewelry they like and for some mysterious reason, simply assume the two will go together. To me, that's like saying if you love pickles and you love hot fudge, a pickle with hot fudge will taste terrific.

Why buy a glittering Bob Mackie design, then spoil the effect by accenting it with a tiny drop necklace? Or an elegantly understated Adolfo, only to pair it with an inappropriately large, showy piece?

Designers do change their collections every season, so it's impossible to give specific advice or absolute rules of what will and won't work. That, after all, is not the point anyway. All clothes, regardless of price tag and label, should be properly accessorized. The purpose of learning about fine jewelry is not simply to make you a more savvy customer — it is to develop a critical sense, an innate feeling for style that can be translated into any area of your life, whatever economic strata you find yourself in. A finely honed sense of style is something you carry with you, whether you ever buy so much as an earring.

But should you find yourself in the market for a designer dress and at the same time find yourself at a loss how to accessorize the look, I've noticed a few basic rules in my work that always come in handy. Again, these tips can be translated into any economic level, lifestyle, and income. And if you're the type who loves whimsy — maybe someone who genuinely likes pickles dipped in hot fudge — throw these hints to the winds. Fashion is self expression, and self expression, above all things, should be fun!

The glitter of a Bob Mackie design is best accented with a dazzling ring and earring.

Glittering and Glamorous

Certain designers are known for their flair for the dramatic.

In outfits created by these designers you don't just walk through a door, you make an entrance. People are going to notice you, and you need jewelry that lets them know you're secure enough to handle the spotlight. Many of these designers create smashing daytime and casual wear as well, but they are best known for their gala gowns, usually employing lots of beading, shimmering fabric, and elaborate trims. Most notable are Fabrice, Oscar de la Renta, Bob Mackie and Zandra Rhodes.

An elaborate necklace only fights with the dress, in this case detracting from the impact of the one-shouldered sweep.

This look is generally opulent and flashy. For this type of clothing, nothing less than showy jewelry will do, preferably a pair of striking earrings, a knock-out ring, and a slightly less glittering bracelet. Because most of these designers employ plunging or elaborate necklines, it's usually best to avoid necklaces. An elaborate necklace only competes with an equally opulent dress rather than accenting it. You want to make a strong, showstopping statement, not a statement that you threw in everything you own because you weren't sure what to wear. On the other hand, and at the risk of sounding contradictory, it's also important not to make the classic mistake of underdressing. If you're bold enough to wear such an outfit, don't second-guess yourself by selecting demure jewels.

I've found most of the glittering and glamorous designers use color liberally, particularly fabulous bright tones. Take care to match or blend your jewelry to the predominant hue. Don't select anything that will clash or look washed out.

Tailored and Tasteful

This type of designer is known for clean lines and uncluttered looks. These clothes, primarily daytime sportswear and short, dressy evening looks, can go almost anywhere. The most notable names among this group are Giorgio Armani, Perry Ellis, Gianfranco Ferre, Anne Klein, Calvin Klein, Karl Lagerfeld, and Ralph Lauren.

The clothing created by these designer houses requires an equally tailored look. Necklaces and earrings are almost always appropriate, but don't overdo it by wearing a ring and bracelet too.

The size of the jewelry is not as important as the type of materials used. Many of these designers like loose, oversized, unconstructed looks. Bulky but plain pieces complement them nicely.

Button or geometric-shaped earrings are better for tailored clothing than more delicate, dangling earrings. Don't use lots of flash and glitter with this clothing. Hold back on the diamonds and strive for more understated stones and looks.

These designers create a sensation quietly. They make an uncomplicated statement, and it's only right to avoid clutter while still providing suitable accents.

Oh-So-Chic

Many designers have made their reputation with flattering, ladylike looks. These clothes attract attention because of their elegance. It's not the glitter or the line of the clothes, but an overall feeling of good taste. Such designers are classicists — never boring, never daring. Their clothes are safe because they're always right. Some of the best known names in the category include Carolina Herrerra, Yves Saint Laurent, James Galanos, Bill Blass, Adolfo, Bernard Perris, Chloe, Chanel, Mary McFadden, and Albert Nipon.

The oh-so-chic outfit, which is most often a luncheon suit, requires elegant, restrained accessories. The clothes speak for themselves, so it's important not to wear too much or too little. Pearls almost always go well with such clothes, and with classic suits, long necklaces can't be beat. Lots of gold is always good because it is simple and elegant — just like these clothes.

A casual look, especially exaggerated styles such as this oversized sweater by Rebecca Moses, calls for large, fun, bold jewelry.

*Adolfo's signature look, with the
unconstructed jacket, looks best with long
chains which complement the suit's long lines.*

Chapter Five

What Jewelry to Wear, When, and Why

No matter how lovely the outfit or how fine the jewelry, if worn inappropriately no one will notice. People will only remember that you were improperly attired, and because we're all trying to put forth our best selves, that's a tremendous waste of time, effort, and money. Never forget that what you are striving for by wearing jewelry is to create your own style, to express yourself at your best and give yourself that added bit of confidence we all need. You are not so much creating an image as expressing it, and learning how to accomplish that is akin to knowing any of the other social amenities that make life a little more gracious, a little more pleasant.

Most women reach into their jewelry box and select what to wear on the spur of the moment. They give little thought to whether the particular piece looks good with a certain outfit, or even if the jewelry is appropriate to the occasion. For many people, jewelry is an afterthought, something dashed on, like perfume, while racing out the door.

Anyone who has ever tried to dress to her best advantage knows it takes more than choosing the right colors or selecting the right styles. Like the courses of a fine meal, every part of an ensemble must complement the other. You must choose not only an outfit that looks stunning but the right occasion to wear that outfit. You must not only select the proper earring for your facial shape, the proper ring for your hand, or the right necklace for your body size, but you must also know how to put those together to their best advantage.

It makes no sense to consider facial shape, body size, coloring, and wardrobe if you don't take the time to pair the jewelry with the appropriate event and style. Such admonitions may sound like common sense, but everyone needs to be reminded of the basics every now and then. And once you have taken the time to analyze what's best for your facial shape, body, and coloring, it's a shame to ruin it by failing to take into account both the play of the clothes and jewelry together, and the etiquette of wearing jewelry.

There are several factors to keep in mind when adorning yourself with jewels, but the basic need is knowing how to combine different types of jewelry appropriately.

That doesn't mean selecting jewelry has to be regimented or dull. On the contrary, I'm a firm believer that jewelry should be synonymous with good times and good feelings. There's nothing more fun than dressing up and there's no better feeling than that of self-confidence. But there is a secret to obtaining that euphoric feeling. It's called good taste, and there's no substitute for it.

Some people may be born with good taste, but most people learn it. If you think no one feels as unsure of themselves as you do, let me reassure you. Many of my most prominent, wealthiest clients are as unsure of themselves as any jewelry neophyte. But with a little practice, and a little common sense, good taste in jewelry — which simply means appropriateness — can become second nature. Once achieved, it leaves the wearer to enjoy the beauty of her jewels and the confidence of knowing they look exactly right.

But again, let me reiterate that nothing is absolute. What's right for most people may be wrong for you — the key is feeling good about yourself.

I've found the biggest problem many women face is knowing how much jewelry to wear. For most people jewelry is a reward, a sign of well-being. There is a natural temptation to show the world how wonderful life is by wearing a lot of jewelry at once.

I have noticed through the years that the more insecure the customer, the more jewelry she wears at once. It's as if they can convince the world they have everything, by flaunting as many pieces as they can squeeze onto an arm, ear, or neck. There is also the common mistake of being afraid to wear much of anything at all, a timidity about making a statement of any kind.

The solution is to strive for a happy medium, a level that conveys to the world that you know what you like and what looks good on you. Don't, for instance, wear several rings on each hand. One ring on either hand, in addition to your wedding rings, is the best rule of thumb. Three rings on two hands are acceptable, but that's the limit. Numerous rings on your fingers look as if you couldn't decide what you liked best, so you decided to wear everything at once.

Similarly, don't wear two earrings on one ear. Some people claim it looks glamorous, but I find it faddish, not fashionable. It's a look for teenagers only, not a classic way to dress.

Two necklaces can look wonderful if they are of the right length. It makes no sense to wear a choker and a long necklace together. Like conflicting traffic signals, the two disparate lengths leave the viewer confused. If you want to wear more than one necklace, wear three or four, properly spaced, or two necklaces, one medium, one long.

The same idea applies to bracelet styles and size. It's ineffective to wear bangle bracelets with flexible bracelets. They fight each other and leave no impression at all, instead of a stylish one. Several large bracelets together also look overdone. Only small or medium sizes look good in large groups. Oversized pieces paired with similarly oversized pieces appear overpowering, no matter how tall you are.

In Europe today it's very chic to combine an elegant evening watch with a small diamond chain. Make sure the bracelet flatters the watch by being simple but elegant, and you have a lovely look for evening. This chic look is fabulous for the right occasion, but don't overdo it by employing it too often.

It's equally important to combine types of materials properly. Don't, for instance, mix costume jewelry and the real thing. I know of one woman who learned this lesson the hard

Prior to World War I, most wrist-watches were worn by women. They were considered effeminate until American Army officers utilized them during the war.

79

way. She was attending a party, wearing every piece of fine jewelry she owned — and a pair of costume earrings. A man she had never seen before approached her and said, "With all the beautiful jewelry you are wearing, you shouldn't be wearing fake earrings." She was appalled at his rudeness, but more irritated that she had afforded him an opportunity to display it.

If you're going to buy fine jewelry, wear it well or not at all. It's better to wear one quality piece, in my opinion, than to obscure its beauty by cluttering it up with other inferior pieces.

Quality is the important thing to keep in mind when combining metals or stones. It's fine, for instance, to wear gold and platinum together, but gold and silver are inappropriate. Silver is known as a less expensive metal, and those who notice such things will find it jarring.

Similarly, mixing stones can add a wonderful effect if done properly. Don't, however, mix jewels of markedly different quality and feeling. Emeralds, diamonds, sapphires and rubies all work well together, but a stunning diamond necklace and a silver turquoise bracelet are wrong. And just because stones are of the same color family is no excuse. An emerald does not belong with a peridot, or a diamond with a white sapphire. It's an insult to a fine stone to pair it with a stone of lesser quality.

The feeling of the jewel is the most important guidepost. It's fabulous to wear a black pearl in one ear and a white pearl in the other, if they match. But to pair a round pearl with an irregularly shaped pearl looks ill-chosen. "Feeling" also applies to cuts of stones. Faceted stones are terrific, and so are cabochon stones, but the two rarely work together. They emote different feelings and succeed only in presenting a mixed message to the viewer.

The same advice holds true for styles of jewelry, too. Occasionally you can combine antique and modern pieces, but more likely than not, it looks awkward. Wearing grandmother's

Ensembles such as these present a lovely solution to the problem of mixing: pair the finest with the finest.

delicate, lacy circle pin with a chunky contemporary necklace gives the impression you reached into a grab bag and put on the first things you found.

With a little thought, these different types of jewelry can all be worn — but not all together at the same time.

There is also the matter of wearing the right jewelry at the right time. Overdressing is the most common worry among my customers, and rightfully so. It's a mistake that involves not just the number of pieces but timing. If you have a business meeting, or a breakfast with friends, don't spoil it by wearing elaborate diamonds. They may be a girl's best friend — but not before lunch. Many people don't feel comfortable wearing them during the day at all, although simple designs are fine for late afternoon. After all, if you wear your best jewels before noon, what will you produce for an encore at midnight? (I do however, love the story of the socialite who said she always entertained her husband at breakfast in diamonds and emeralds — and nothing else!)

Similarly, you should not wear your simple, everyday drop necklace with an evening gown. And an everyday watch, be it leather or even a heavy watch with diamonds, is inappropriate for evening. Remember, you're striving for an overall look, not a hodgepodge. Ask yourself what image you're trying to convey, then carry that out through every aspect of dressing, from clothes to jewelry, makeup, and accessories.

It's nice to get lots of use out of your jewels, but jewelry is fun because it's special. Don't waste their impact by wearing them at the wrong time. There's an unwritten rule in New York: don't wear even the simplest of jewels on the subway or down crowded streets. They may provide too great a temptation for a thief, who can disappear into the crowd easily. For the same reason, don't wear your fine gems while exercising, for instance, or to the beauty shop.

By wearing jewels to the beauty shop you run the risk of

damaging them with chemicals or hair spray. You also may leave them behind accidentally. And it's unwise to wear jewelry while exercising because it may be easily lost or tempt passing thieves as you jog by. Also, I advise against it because you may damage your body. Earrings, for instance, can stretch the earlobe when worn during strenuous exercise and long necklaces can be dangerous when working out.

Sometimes women simply don't know what to do with certain jewelry items. They may have a pin they love, but the neckline of their dress is inappropriate. So they place it on their fur, which is totally wrong. In the first place, it's not only ostentatious but dangerous, both to the fur, which may be damaged, and to the pin, which may be lost.

Gloves and rings also present a similar problem. If you want to wear gloves, don't wear rings on top of them. It's a bad look. In this instance it's best to choose what item is more important to you to wear, but don't make the mistake of trying to wear both.

The key to dressing right, simply put, is suitability. No one can mistake the elegance of a beautiful piece when properly displayed — in the right setting, at the right time, accompanied by the correct clothes and other jewels. Nature has created items of great beauty — it's up to you to display them properly.

Chapter Six
Assembling a Jewelry Wardrobe

If you've become as entranced with beautiful gems as I am, you're anxious to make that first purchase. Hopefully you've taken stock of your features and decided what to play up and what to minimize by analyzing your facial shape, body shape and size, coloring, and the type and color of clothes in your closet. If so, you're ready to embark on one of the most exciting adventures I know — buying beautiful jewels of your very own.

The excitement of collecting fine jewels is one of the most fun aspects of buying jewelry, but it's also important not to get too caught up, too carried away. It takes time to assemble a jewelry wardrobe. Collecting fine jewels requires the same approach as assembling a quality clothing wardrobe. Decide what your needs are and in what order of importance, then accumulate those items through the years. It's tempting, once you've become enamored with beautiful jewels, to want to buy as many as you can afford at once. But remember, these gems have been around for thousands of years, and they will be around for thousands more. It takes time and thought to acquire the pieces that are just right for you, the ones that will afford you infinite pleasure through the years. It's crucial that you assemble a basic wardrobe, then build on it with time.

Though I advise buying timeless looks more often than not, there is definitely a place in any jewelry wardrobe for the occasional whimsical, trendy item. But those should be purchased after the basics have been acquired. And should you tire of those items in the future, or if they fall out of fashion, you can always have them redone into something you prefer.

Metals

As I mentioned earlier, the best jewelry is made of 18-karat gold because it is more durable than gold of a higher karat content and more beautiful than 14-karat. To make sure you're getting what you pay for, always ask to see the stamp that

Different finishes greatly alter the look of a metal as illustrated here in these classic bracelets.

shows the metal content. By law, gold and silver jewelry must be stamped with quality marks noting the content. An 18-karat piece will be stamped "18k," unless it is imported from Europe, when it will bear the number "750." A 14-karat piece will be stamped "14k" or "585."

If you do opt for silver jewelry, insist on sterling. The word "sterling" assures that the item is 92.5 percent silver. Platinum is also a popular metal but, unfortunately, there is no universal stamp for platinum, which makes it difficult to identify without testing.

When you are ready to buy, you will find you have not only numerous materials to choose from but also many finishes. The polished finish, a glossy bright look, is popular as is the satin, which is a softer, slightly burnished look.

Other common finishes include the Florentine, which is delicate, with many tiny lines; and two more contemporary looks, the hammered, which looks exactly as it sounds, and the bark finish, a rough, clunky look suitable only for oversized pieces.

Once you have familiarized yourself with what is available in the marketplace, it's wise to have a basic plan for purchasing jewelry. I suggest buying a watch first, simply because it is the most functional item. Follow that with a pair of gold earrings, a ring, a necklace, and a bracelet. Diamonds should be the first "stone" purchased, with pearls following quickly, then those gems which best complement your coloring.

Watches

Most jewelry pieces are ornamental, not functional. The wristwatch is the sole exception, so naturally a watch should be purchased first. Many people tend to overlook watches when discussing jewelry, but a watch is the piece you look at most often and the one most visible to others as well.

A lady's first watch should be a relatively inexpensive, casual style with a leather band. Lizard and alligator skins are appropriate in neutral tones of brown and black. If you can afford it, a solid gold band is wonderful, but that doubles or triples the price.

The shape of the watch face depends on your wrist size, but the popular classic is the tank style watch, the design made famous by Cartier. (The tank style watch is a geometric shape that resembles the silhouette of the first American tanks to appear in World War I; its design was a tribute to the American tank corps commanders who helped defend France.) The face should be basic — gold with dots, preferably — a look which blends nicely but doesn't appear flashy.

Quartz movements are highly touted today, but I don't think they are any match for the craftsmanship of the master watchmaker. You're buying quality, not simply convenience, and the old-fashioned mechanical watches are impossible to improve upon. Mechanical movements are still made completely by hand, not machine. While both types keep time equally well, I find an inexplicable feeling of satisfaction comes from owning a watch that works in the "time-honored" tradition. Part of the charm of owning jewelry is that you are buying the fruits of someone's talent, someone's creativity, and that extends not only to gem cutters or jewelry designers but to master watchmakers as well. A mechanical movement may require added care since it needs to be cleaned more frequently, but the workmanship is unparalleled. Look for the word "mechanical" or "automatic" instead of "quartz."

Regardless of the type of movement, however, any fine watch should be water-resistant and shock-proof. An everyday watch is going to get a lot of use and abuse; for practical reasons it's unwise to put much money into a watch that cannot be durable as well as attractive.

Very elegant dress watches won't come with these features, but they are not necessary because an evening watch is not meant to be worn daily. But because evening watches are extremely expensive, and worn only on occasion, don't purchase one until you have assembled a fairly extensive jewelry wardrobe.

Earrings

A watch may be the most visible piece of jewelry, but it's not always the most noticed. As I have discussed before, that honor belongs to the earring, which should be your next major purchase. A watch should be your first purchase because of the function it serves, but earrings run a close second because of the personal fashion statement they make.

The size and shape of an earring depends on your face and earlobe, but that first pair should be made of plain gold, not of gems or multicolored metal. This is the pair of earrings you will wear daily, not just for special occasions, so it must be extremely versatile. In all probability it will be a simple geometric shape, a button or oval, depending on your needs.

Unlike the leather-banded watch, this piece can make the transition from day into evening without too much trouble. If you want to dress up but can't afford a pair of diamond or precious-stone earrings, some jewelers are now making "jackets" which can be mixed and matched to increase the versatility of the plain earring. But when dramatic evening earrings become necessary to your lifestyle, the best bet by far is a pair of diamond studs. After making that purchase, buy whichever stones look best with your coloring and wardrobe.

When buying earrings, always shake your head to see if adjustment is necessary. They should fit tightly enough so you don't have to worry about losing them, but should never feel painful or uncomfortable. Always try both earrings on, because no two ears are alike and they should look flattering from both sides. Also, if you frequently wear hats, always try the earrings on with a hat. Earrings can look quite different with a hairstyle swept back to accommodate a hat than they do when worn with your normal hairstyle.

The shape of your first pair of earrings depends on your facial characteristics, but basic gold should be the metal of choice.

Rings

Once a watch and earrings have been purchased, a simple ring should be your next buy. Many people are anxious to buy necklaces, but remember that necks are often covered up by clothing and a neck does not call attention to itself. Hands are constantly moving and usually uncovered. They're quickly noticed and should be featured accordingly.

Engagement and wedding rings are generally the first rings worn by women, but it's also nice to have a more fashionable, less classic ring. A plain gold ring, usually a domed shape, is a good beginning. Worn on the fourth finger of the right hand, it makes an attractive, quiet statement. Such a ring is best worn during the day, but can be worn for casual evenings as well.

When buying a ring try it on, not just for looks, but for comfort. To insure a good fit, measure the length of the inside of your knuckle and buy only what allows you to move your finger freely.

Necklaces

A gold necklace, selected to flatter your facial shape and size, is a basic for any wardrobe. This is a piece you can have more fun with however. You won't wear it every day because not every neckline allows it, so it provides a better opportunity to express your uniqueness than other pieces. A necklace doesn't have to go as many places as a watch, earrings, or ring, so by all means look for something unusual.

At one time, the rope was a classic necklace, but today it's considered passe, with more women opting for a choker or collar length, depending on what complements their face. Some necklaces fill both roles, however, being doubled to wear as a choker or worn full-length for a longer look.

When buying necklaces for a special occasion or a specific outfit, I recommend trying the clothes and jewelry on together before making a final decision. If necessary, take the clothes or

The first known engagement ring was bestowed on Mary of Burgundy in 1477, a gift from Archduke Maximilian of Austria.

the jewelry to the store. Do make the effort, because the necklace is worn closer to the clothing than any other piece of jewelry and can make or break an outfit. It may take a little more time and trouble, but you'll know immediately if the necklace is right.

I've mentioned previously the importance of taking into account the length of the neck when buying necklaces, but there are other factors to consider as well, such as sagging skin or scars.

Older women who are disturbed by sagging skin often feel they should avoid necklaces completely. While it's best not to accent problem areas, necklaces need not be dropped from anyone's wardrobe altogether. No one expects anyone to age without showing the effects at least slightly.

A strand of pearls or a loose choker is a good solution for the aging neck because it is tasteful without being flashy. Large pieces are fine if they don't look weighty, but it's best to stay away from the extremely heavy, ornate necklace. Such necklaces are designed not merely to flatter but to draw attention, which is not the purpose when the neck isn't an area you wish to dramatize.

If the skin is a real problem, I advise staying away from pieces that encircle the neck and recommend longer necklaces over a high-collared blouse.

Bracelets

The first bracelet you buy should undoubtedly be a classic bangle. It's a wearable, versatile style that shows quiet good taste. A single bangle looks silly, however — buy at least two, more if they're very thin. The width and number should be adjusted to your size of course. The first bangle bracelet is best if it's a simple gold design, but other good buys include bangles set with cabochon stones, particularly some of the opaque stones that go well with many types of clothes and colors.

After you have purchased a classic bangle for everyday wear, consider one of the jeweled variety.

Delicate chains, for either necklaces or bracelets, have been so popular in recent years that the market is glutted. I advise against purchasing such necklaces because they are not only common, but they don't wear well, often getting tangled and looking messy instead of chic. Don't be attracted by special prices on such bracelets — if it's a tired look, it won't look good no matter how inexpensive it is.

After you've purchased the basic pieces, you can turn your attention to buying beautiful gems. This for me is the most thrilling part of collecting jewelry — the chance to act as the steward of one of nature's most beautiful creations. It's also fabulous to realize you can place a gem in the setting of your choice, but if the next person to own it does not like it, you have not taken away from its beauty as it can simply be reset for someone else to their liking. No other art form can make quite the same claim, and to me that's one of the great marvels of jewelry.

The first stones you purchase should unquestionably be diamonds, and for one simple reason: they are the most neutral and thus the easiest to match with any clothing or other jewelry.

In my opinion, the important rule to remember when buying diamonds is not to buy anything tiny. A very small diamond makes no statement — other than the fact that you could not afford to buy anything larger. That doesn't mean you have to buy a huge stone, but I advise saving your money until you can afford at least a half carat. If it's smaller than that, no one will notice and one of the purposes of owning beautiful jewelry — to convey your image effectively — is lost.

There are four elements to consider when purchasing diamonds: color, cut, clarity, and carat weight. As mentioned before, most diamonds are clear white or colorless. A poor quality diamond has a yellowish tinge, which is not desirable, but these inferior stones must not be confused with "fancy" diamonds, those rare stones which are naturally colored yellow

The older woman looks best in a longer necklace which does not draw attention to the neck area.

Weighty pieces which fit closely around the neck are not always flattering.

or several other colors. Diamond colors are graded from D to Z, with D representing the finest on the scale. It is not necessary, or even possible, to always buy a D color diamond — what you are willing to spend and what quality level you desire are entirely matters of personal preference.

The cut of a diamond simply describes the shape in which the stone has been cut. In their rough form, diamonds are less than impressive, usually resembling a grayish lump. What sets them afire is the art of cutting. There are several basic cuts, and a good diamond cutter shapes a stone according to what will best display its beauty.

Perhaps the most famous story of cutting a diamond is that of the legendary diamond cutter from Amsterdam, Joseph Asscher. This highly regarded cutter was given the enviable task (or unenviable task, depending on your point of view!) of cutting the famous Cullinan Diamond. The Cullinan weighed 3,601 carats, and Asscher spent months studying the lines of cleavage in the huge stone.

When the moment of truth came, Asscher's hand reportedly shook and he broke into a nervous sweat. The mallet fell against the steel rule — and the rule broke in half but the diamond remained intact! Asscher went to the hospital to recover from the ordeal, then took his physician with him when the time came to attempt the cutting a second time. Fortunately for his health — and reputation — the diamond broke cleanly in two, exactly along the lines Asscher had envisioned. The poor man did not discover his success until some time later — he fainted when he struck the stone!

The third element after color and cut, the clarity of a diamond, indicates the number of flaws it contains. To describe a diamond as "flawless" means it has no spots, cracks, or inclusions visible under 10-power magnification. The most commonly used clarity system uses the initials VV, V, S, and I to rate the presence of flaws. The initials stand for Very, Very;

Very; Slight or Small; and Inclusion or Imperfect.

You need not insist on a flawless stone. In fact, many lovely stones are far from perfect. Obviously, the fewer the flaws the better the quality — and the higher the price.

The weight of a diamond is measured in carats, a term that originally referred to the name of the seed from the carob tree, which was used as a measure. A carat weighs .007 of an ounce and is divided into 100 points. A ten-point diamond represents one-tenth of a carat.

The larger the diamond, the rarer it is, and the more expensive, of course. But don't be deceived into buying a diamond, just because it's large. A big stone of poor quality is worth less than a smaller stone of greater beauty. A general rule of thumb, not just with weight but with all aspects of a diamond, is to buy the best you can afford — and, if possible, afford nothing but the best!

After purchasing your first diamonds, it's best to add pearls to your wardrobe. I haven't met a woman yet who didn't adore pearls. These simple gems can dress up a plain dress or, like the bangle bracelet, can go almost anywhere. They speak softly but forcefully of good taste.

The elegant multi-stranded wristwatch is of 3 mm. cultured pearls. The ring and earrings below, all large lush South Sea pearls.

Unlike most other highly-valued gems, pearls don't result from an organic process or upheaval in the earth's depths. They are a gift from the sea, the product of an animal trying to defend itself. All pearls, saltwater, fresh-water, and cultured, come from the same place of origin — the inside of a mollusk, usually an oyster.

When a foreign body is imbedded inside the mollusk, the animal protects itself from the intruder by coating the body with a smooth film of nacre, which reduces the irritation. The pearl grows by layers, generally taking from one to three years to form. Pearls from inside the body of an oyster are the most valued because they are more perfectly round than those attached to the shell.

95

The best pearls have few blemishes and a strong lustre or ability to reflect light. The lustre, or orient of a pearl as it is sometimes called, looks almost as if there is a soft glow from inside.

There is nothing quite so wonderful as a lovely strand of natural pearls, but the majority of pearls today are cultured pearls, those made by nature with a little push from mankind. Cultured pearls were first introduced in 1896 by a Japanese gentleman named Mikimoto. Others had tried for centuries to induce pearl production in mollusks, but it was Mikimoto who succeeded by inserting a small seed pearl into an oyster shell, then returning the oyster to the water for 18 months to three years.

Efforts to duplicate other gems have been unsuccessful, but Mikimoto's work with pearls has proved so effective and popular, even experts are hard pressed to tell the difference without extensive testing. Cultured pearls are not simulated pearls — they are real, but man gives nature a little boost to stimulate production! Cultured pearls are readily accepted as fine jewelry, and like natural pearls they do not come cheaply.

After purchasing your first diamonds and pearls, determining which stone to collect next is strictly a matter of what meets your needs. Whatever that stone is, have fun!

Caring for Your Jewelry

People who spend thousands of dollars on a car never dream of letting it go for months without a tuneup or, at the very least, a good wash and wax. But they'll spend even more money on fine jewelry and never bother to have it cleaned or checked for needed repairs.

I ran into comedian Phyllis Diller once, almost a dozen years after selling her a diamond ring with stones that moved in a circle around the setting. She recognized me and mentioned that the ring no longer "worked," the stones no longer moved freely. I asked when she had last cleaned it, and to my horror she replied that she never had. When she sent me the ring for examination, I discovered the stones no longer moved because the setting was clogged with dirt.

I cleaned the ring and returned it to Ms. Diller, and later received a letter expressing her pleasure over her "new" ring.

Just like furniture or cars or clothes, jewelry gets dirty. Natural skin oils and makeup rub off on pieces worn close to the skin, in addition to the usual everyday dust any object collects. Though few people bother, fine jewelry should be cleaned once a month. Why own something beautiful if you cannot show it to full advantage?

That's not to say I recommend cleaning your gems yourself. On the contrary, I strongly suggest taking your jewelry to an expert. Through the years, many home remedies have been concocted for cleaning gems, and instead of helping, most of them are potentially harmful. Ammonia and soap, for instance, may appear to clean the jewel, but in reality they often leave a film that dulls its appearance. Boiling jewelry in water, another popular home remedy, is not only ineffective but dangerous. Sudden heat or cold may damage the stone or metal and result in an avoidable loss.

Some jewelers give or sell customers a jar of cleaning solution, but it's still advisable to have jewelry cleaned professionally. Remember, you paid for service as well as the jewelry itself, so your jeweler won't be offended. In fact, he'll be glad to see you taking care of the gems he loves so much!

A fine jeweler will not only clean the piece free of charge, he will also check it for loose stones or prongs showing wear. Because he checks each piece, he can employ an ultrasonic cleaning machine. Such gadgets are available for home use, but I don't recommend them because stones may fall out in the machine if a prong is loose. For the same reason, I do not recommend using brushes to remove dirt. Brushing often loosens settings and may result in a tragic loss.

Platinum is five times as rare as gold. To produce enough platinum for one engagement and wedding band, it requires 30 cubic yards of ore — nearly half the size of a railroad boxcar.

If you do clean your jewels at home, make sure you have a cleaning solution suitable to the job. Pearls, for instance, cannot be cleaned along with other jewels because they are sensitive to chemicals. In fact, while all jewelry requires some tender loving care, few need it more than pearls.

For best results, pearls should be wiped off with a clean, slightly damp cloth after every wearing. It's also wise to take pains to avoid spraying pearls with perfume, hair spray, or any liquid containing alcohol because such liquids may ruin the pearl's lustre or cause it to peel.

When putting pearls away, place them in a soft pouch or container where they will occasionally be exposed to air. Do not put them in sealed plastic bags or even closed boxes in the dark. Pearls improve with use, so it's best to take them out and wear them often.

One of the most important parts of caring for pearls is maintaining the stringing. The cord, which should be made of silk and knotted between each pearl, stretches with time, and may break. If the necklace or bracelet appears to be loosening, restring them immediately. I advise doing this at least once a year, sometimes twice. There's nothing sadder than losing a beautiful object that gives you pleasure, and if this step isn't taken, pearls can be easily lost.

In recent years, as the value of jewels has risen sharply and people have grown more fearful of losing or having their gems stolen, some collectors have stashed their jewelry in safety deposit boxes and refused to wear them.

I can think of no sadder mistake. What after all is the sense of owning one of the most beautiful, incredible creations on earth and hiding it in a dark metal box? Jewelry is like any object of art — without an audience to marvel and appreciate its beauty, it has no value, no meaning. To me, there is no sense in collecting jewelry if you're not going to wear it and derive pleasure from the beauty it gives you and others.

Only about 20 percent of all the diamonds mined can be used for jewelry.

I feel equally bad about the trend to wearing synthetic jewels, copies of the real thing. Just as a clever forgery is no substitute for great art, there simply is no substitute for real gems. I've always enjoyed the story of the wealthy Houston dowager who, when asked whether she worried about thieves stealing the huge diamond butterfly pin jauntily fastened to her evening gown, replied, "Oh, my dear, if I'm going to be hit over the head for something, I'd much rather it be the real thing!"

I have another customer who says, "I would wear the Hope Diamond — if Lloyd's of London were going along with me!"

No one should dwell on the thought of being the victim of crime, but I admire the willingness of these women to settle for nothing but the best. If you take appropriate precautions, there is no reason why you cannot wear your fine jewelry as it was meant to be worn — often and with joy.

Appropriate precautions include, of course, insurance. Insurance needs can be summed up succinctly: make sure you have it. Fine jewelry is not automatically included in most policies, so each piece should be listed separately and covered adequately.

For insurance purposes, every fine piece should be appraised by a reputable jeweler. Before taking any new purchase home, make sure you have obtained an appraisal from your jeweler. Generally such an appraisal will be a GIA (Gemological Institute of America) form, including an exact description with such information as metal content, carat weights of individual stones and combined weight, and purchase price.

Appraisals should be updated annually to enable you to increase your insurance if necessary. Most fine jewelers will gladly provide an updated appraisal. If you misplace the appraisal and the jewelry does need to be replaced, contact your jeweler immediately. He should have accurate records and can

advise you on replacement value at no charge.

Some jewelers also provide customers with a photograph of the piece, which can be helpful if replacement is necessary.

It's sad that such measures are necessary, but in my opinion it's a small price to pay for the privilege of owning beautiful gems. After all, life is meant to be enjoyed, and there are few joys comparable to collecting one of nature's finest gifts. It's a tragedy to keep beauty hidden, and if you can afford to own fine jewelry, you can't afford not to enjoy it. Wear your jewels often, with pride and joy — you're doing yourself and others a favor by displaying one of the marvels of nature.

Certainly, there is nothing to match the real thing.

Chapter Seven
Buying Jewelry with Confidence

Though the history of beautiful gems dates back to the beginning of time, the history of master jewelers is a much shorter chronicle. Only in the last few centuries have the techniques of metal work, gem cutting, and design been elevated to the art form these dazzling materials deserve. If there is any doubt about jewelers qualifying as artists, consider that several of the most renowned artists began as apprentices to jewelers, including Donatello and Botticelli.

But only in the last 100 years or so have certain jewelers risen to legendary status, known for their reputations not simply as purveyors of beautiful goods but as creators, artists of the highest order. Many of these jewelry "houses" are still in existence today, and though their original founders have long since passed away and the companies have often been sold out of the family, their reputations endure. That is one of the most important aspects of doing business as a jeweler: reputation. It speaks of professionalism, artistry, and quality, and is something anyone buying gems for either pleasure or investment must consider carefully. But before searching for a reputable jeweler yourself, it's helpful to consider those who have made enormous contributions to the jewelry business as a whole, as well as earning great personal acclaim.

In my opinion, the most influential jewelers in recent history include Faberge, Harry Winston, Tiffany, Cartier, Bulgari, and the new kid on the block, Graff, from London. Each occupies a special niche, a spot they have carved out by virtue of their sterling reputation year in and year out. There are many other fine jewelers, and reputations come and go; but for what they have meant to my profession in the past, their contributions should be acknowledged by anyone seeking an appreciation of beautiful gems.

Ironically, the one man hailed unanimously as a master craftsman had little interest in jewelry itself but an overwhelming obsession with gems and metals. His name was

Bulgari. Heart-shaped emeralds surrounded by diamonds set in 18 karat gold. Part of a four piece set.

Cartier. Carved emerald and oriental pearl and diamond necklace, of Indian inspiration.

Peter Carl Faberge, but he is known today simply as Faberge.

Faberge was the court jeweler to the last ruling czars of Russia. He assumed control of his family's jewelry business in 1870, at the young age of 24, and promptly shifted the emphasis from traditional jewelry pieces to objects of art. The house of Faberge was soon patronized by members of the Russian ruling family, but it was not until 1883 that Faberge originated what he has become most famous for: fabulous jeweled Easter eggs.

That year, Faberge recommended to Czar Alexander III that he bestow a jeweled egg on his wife for the holiday instead of the traditional piece of jewelry. He promised a special surprise for the Czar. When the time came, Faberge presented him with a plain white enamel egg — but inside was a gold yolk, and inside the yolk was a tiny chicken of different-colored golds. Inside the chicken was a model of the Imperial crown, and inside the crown was a tiny egg-shaped ruby. The Czar was so pleased by the unusual gift, that he ordered one every year, a tradition continued by his son, Nicholas II. Over the years, Faberge produced at least 57 such treasures, which are now highly sought collectors items.

Two great ironies stand out when discussing the work of this master craftsman: he served primarily as a catalyst, overseeing the work of others, rather than executing it himself, and despite his ornate works, Faberge was a believer in understatement. At one time he employed more than 700 craftsmen, producing a wide range of items, from icons, clocks, boxes, and trays, to cups, fans, clocks — anything which could be jeweled.

Faberge came to the attention of the world in 1900 when his work was displayed at the World's Fair in Paris. Prior to his impact on jewels of the day, nineteenth century jewelry was large and cumbersome. He delighted in delicate, dainty items, and, while using every known stone in his creations, he almost always employed cabochon cuts instead of brilliant cuts, which he considered vulgar.

Faberge was aware that his approach to jewelry as art was dramatically different from that of other jewelers. In 1914, he commented on the prominent jeweler-retailers of his time when he said, "These people are merchants and not artist-jewelers. Expensive things interest me little if the value is merely in so many diamonds and pearls."

At about the same time Faberge's father was establishing his family business, another family in France was beginning a legendary jewelry company known as Cartier. Begun in 1847 by Louis-Francois Cartier, it reached its zenith in the early part of the twentieth century when the firm received no less than 15 letters appointing Cartier as official purveyor to various royal households, from King Edward VII to King Zog of Albania.

Cartier was instrumental in the trend to consider jewelry as fashion, since the firm viewed the work of Paris' top designers as a background for their beautiful gems. Like Faberge, Cartier produced many decorative objects as well as jewelry, but the company is best known for their contributions to twentieth-century design, including that of incorporating an understanding of the Orient into their famous art deco pieces.

In 1881, another legendary jewelry house was founded, an Italian company called Bulgari. Sotirio Bulgari fled to Italy from Greece during the time of the Turkish massacres in his country. After a brief period in Naples, he settled in Rome, where he began his career selling silver trinkets at the top of the Spanish Steps. Trained as a master silversmith, he soon parlayed his expertise into what is today one of the world's most renowned companies, with stores on the Via Condotti in Rome, and also in Paris, Geneva, Monte Carlo, and New York. Though Bulgari also produces many whimsical novelty items, they are known for their use of ancient coins in heavy gold linked necklaces and cabochon stones.

Cartier. Symbol of Cartier renown, the panther, here constructed of platinum, diamonds, and onyx.

Though most of the world's renowned jewelers were

found in Europe in the nineteenth century, an equally prestigious business was founded in the U.S. at about the same time: Tiffany & Company.

Charles Tiffany opened his stationery and gift shop in 1837, but within a matter of years, the store became known for its jewelry. It was Tiffany that brought the sterling silver standard to the U.S., and Tiffany which created the six-pronged setting for diamond solitaires now known as a "Tiffany" setting.

Harry Winston. Diamond necklace created in 1980 contains 283 diamonds weighing 163 carats.

In recent years the store has made a significant contribution to the acceptance of jewelry as both art and fashion by working with name jewelry designers such as Angela Cummings, Paloma Picasso, Jean Schlumberge, and Elsa Peretti. Tiffany does not deal in costume jewelry or plated items, but they have succeeded in crafting lovely items from sterling, a material most jewelers do not work with.

Though Tiffany has a well-deserved reputation, another American was long revered as the ultimate jeweler: Harry Winston.

Compared to other renowned jewelers, Harry Winston is a relative newcomer. He founded the company that bears his name in 1932, after working in the business for several years. Through the years he handled some of the most famous stones in history, including the Hope Diamond, which Winston donated to the Smithsonian Institution as a gift to the people of the United States.

Winston's influence was also important because he helped change the emphasis in jewelry design from the typical heavy settings to fine, hand-made, flexible wire settings known for their fluidity, grace, and dimensionality.

The House of Graff, founded by Laurence Graff, has only been in business about 25 years, it but has already been recognized for its contributions to the industry, and sought out by celebrities and royalty around the world. Graff is known for handling many of the large, historic stones and cutting them into virtually flawless gems. Many of their designs are large, stunning looks that attract a prominent clientele.

Just because these firms have become prominent however, does not mean they are the only fine jewelers in the world. On the contrary, there are many, many outstanding jewelers, some with large companies, some with relatively small concerns. You need not deal with a major "name" to acquire lovely gems, but you must find a reputable jeweler, one you feel comfortable with.

The old adage that you get what you pay for is never more applicable than it is in the jewelry business. After all, you are paying not just for metal and stones but for design, creativity, reputation, and service. You are buying a work of art, and just as you would not buy a costly painting from a street vendor, you should not buy jewels from just anyone.

Any jeweler, no matter how big or small, deals with millions of dollars worth of merchandise daily. Many of my best customers have spent more money with me at my salon than they have anywhere else, including their real estate broker, automobile dealer, or even their stockbroker. They must, and do, trust me implicitly as someone who not only knows but loves the dazzling creations produced by nature and man working together. My customers are aware I earn my living by selling these beautiful pieces to them, but they also know that by making them happy, I stand to profit more in the future. And matching a beautiful gem to a happy owner, gives me a tremendous feeling of satisfaction.

Therefore, I am obviously appalled by the number of people who simply stroll into a neighborhood jeweler to do business, without giving the matter any thought whatsoever. No astute businessman or woman would buy stock, bonds, or an automobile without being fully aware of whom they were dealing with and their reputation in the community. Fine

Graff. Heart-shaped diamond necklace weighing 67.90 carats with Le Grand Coeur d'Afrique, 70.03 carats and Le Petit Coeur d'Afrique, 25.22 carats. Total weight, 163.15 carats.

jewelry often represents an even larger investment in both money and pleasure.

The best way to find a reputable jeweler is through word of mouth. I don't recommend broadcasting your intentions to purchase large pieces of jewelry to the world at large, but I do suggest asking friends discreetly to advise you about a jeweler's reputation. Inquire about his merchandise selection and quality, the service he offers, and any policies that may affect your purchase. If you are new in town and don't know anyone to ask, by all means request a list of satisfied clients from the jeweler you are considering doing business with. If he has been in business for several years, he should have plenty of satisfied customers. If not, you don't want to deal with him.

It's also a good idea to check with the Better Business Bureau. The BBB can tell you if there have been any serious problems or complaints lodged against the company. If you are interested in buying a piece away from home, follow the same suggestions — especially if you are buying in another country. It's extremely easy to get taken away from home. Be careful.

Whether at home or abroad, I cannot stress enough the importance of not buying tremendous "values." Avoid those jewelers who advertise special sales or exceptionally low prices and those claiming to be wholesalers. Most fine jewelers do not hold regular sales — Tiffany & Company has held only two sales in its 148-year history, and those were held strictly because of a change in ownership. There are fair prices when buying jewelry but there are no "bargains." If a jeweler advertises low prices, he is cutting corners somewhere, and if it's not in the quality of the merchandise, it's in the service. That may not seem important the day you buy the jewelry but it becomes more of a factor when you need prompt service, repairs, appraisals, or any kind of special aid.

After you have worked with a jeweler for a number of years and feel extremely comfortable with him, you may be able

Elizabeth, the wife of Emperor Franz Josef of Austria, usually wore a ruby as a talisman, but legend has it she failed to wear it on the day she was assassinated.

to let him buy pieces for you. Otherwise, never, never buy a piece without seeing it first, and that applies to both catalogs and advertising in print or on television. Looks can be deceiving, and it never hurts to take the time to examine a piece closely before buying.

If you have asked people you trust to recommend a jeweler and have several firms to choose from, give them all a chance by comparison shopping. Visit each salon, look at the inventory, talk to the personnel. When you find a jeweler who seems particularly attuned to your needs, someone with whom you feel at ease, take your business there.

I cannot emphasize enough the personal nature of dealing with a jeweler. It's not simply a financial matter like purchasing stocks or bonds, nor is buying jewelry merely a matter of personal taste like shopping for clothes. You are buying an expensive, lasting piece of art and craftsmanship, which will give you pleasure and may also result in a monetary gain through normal value appreciation. You must deal with someone you trust and with whom you feel comfortable or the pleasure of buying beautiful jewels is diminished.

The jeweler that is right for you may not be right for someone else. Some customers prefer to be left alone to decide what they like best; others prefer more direction and advice. The most common complaint from my clients is that jewelers are condescending or appear to be more interested in making a sale than in looking out for their best interests.

Any fine jeweler should answer questions gladly, without making you feel intimidated. Never be afraid to ask. After all the reason you seek out a reputable jeweler is because you want to deal with someone who can reassure you about the purchase you are contemplating. There is no stupid question; the only stupid question is the one not asked. If you are unsure what type of stone you're looking at, ask. If you are not sure about the metal content, inquire. If you don't understand why one piece is more costly than another, there is nothing wrong with asking why. A jeweler loves a knowledgeable customer because that customer has a greater understanding and appreciation of his work.

If you are not knowledgeable, he should be happy to inform you. And no one should buy jewelry without being informed. If the jeweler is vague or unable to answer your questions to your satisfaction, I recommend taking your business elsewhere. Never forget you are buying jewelry for fun, and if the experience of purchasing the long awaited item is not pleasurable, there's no sense in pursuing it. Looking at beautiful gems and learning about them is half the fun of buying and collecting. The actual ownership is the most fun of all, but don't forget: just as a journey includes more than arriving at a destination, buying jewelry involves more than taking a piece home.

Whether you prefer close attention or the chance to contemplate jewelry on your own, you should never feel pressured into buying hastily. No matter if you plan to spend $1,000 or $5,000,000, this is a large purchase for you. You must be happy with it and if you are, you will probably return to do business again. Subsequent purchases are usually higher in price, so it's to the jeweler's advantage to be sure you make the right selection.

Do not buy anything until you have satisfied your curiosity by viewing everything the jeweler has in stock. You may have a specific style in mind, but he may be able to suggest an alternative you may like better. Remember that the price tag includes his expertise, and if you trust him, suggestions should be welcome.

Many wonderful jewels come with matching pieces, such as earrings and necklaces. Don't feel you must buy an ensemble at once. It's not necessary to buy everything together. That, in fact, is one of the fun parts of collecting jewelry — adding to your wardrobe through the years, and pairing today's diamond with yesterday's emerald. Buy what you like, when you can afford it — not necessarily an entire ensemble that may not fit into your budget, much less your lifestyle.

Once a particular piece catches your eye, don't hesitate to try it on. No matter how exquisite the jewelry, you are not buying it to display in a museum. It is meant to be worn and enjoyed, and will not sit forever on a flat piece of black velvet. Jewelry looks entirely different swinging from an ear or neck than it does in a display case. Try it on, check your appearance, see if you like the way it feels.

If you don't see something that appeals to you, ask what else the jeweler has in stock. Most jewelers keep an inventory larger than their display space. He may have just what you're looking for, but it may not be in sight. Even if he doesn't have it in stock, he may be able to locate a piece from another source quickly. Give him a chance to earn his commission — and your confidence.

Ensembles, such as this crystal and ruby watch and necklace, make lovely sets; but don't feel you must buy everything at once. Buy what you want and what you can afford.

Once you have established a mutual trust, some fine jewelers will allow you to take items home to think about before committing yourself. Do not expect a large chain operation to extend this courtesy, but if you have worked with a jeweler long enough to have established a rapport, it's entirely possible. You may be asked to give a check or credit card as a sign of good faith, which also simplifies the procedure if you do decide to purchase the piece after you've had a chance to think about it. If the piece is not right for you and you decide against buying it, return it to the jeweler the next day. This enables him to offer it to other customers. Keeping it for a longer time, is not only discourteous but damaging as he is losing potential income. When the piece is returned, your check will be returned or the credit slip destroyed, and you can continue looking for something you like better.

Sometimes you may know exactly what you want, but the

jeweler may not have anything like it. In that case, custom ordering may be your best solution. You should be willing to spend a minimum of $1,000 for custom work — and some time. Custom work costs 25 to 40 percent more than pieces already in stock because of the added design work involved, so be certain the additional expense is worth it to you. For many, getting exactly what they want makes the additional expense a small price to pay, but it is a factor you should consider.

When ordering a custom piece, be prepared to place a deposit of 20 to 50 percent. Just as an interior decorator needs assurance that you sincerely intend to purchase the materials you're ordering, a jeweler needs to know this is not a passing fancy.

Explain what you want to the jeweler, being as specific as possible. Describe not only the design, but the materials. He will submit a detailed design for your inspection within a few days. If you like the design but aren't sure, you can ask for a wax model, which generally takes two to four weeks.

Once the model satisfies you, give the jeweler the go-ahead and be prepared to wait another month for the final product. It may take longer, depending on the availability of the materials you've requested and the detail work required. Some stones, for instance, are harder to find than others, particularly in larger sizes.

Though you are understandably anxious, try not to rush the jeweler. It takes at least seven professionals to make a piece of jewelry, so it's almost impossible to do it quickly. Your patience will be rewarded when the finished piece meets your expectations.

Custom work is not limited to totally new pieces. You can also take advantage of the jeweler's services for updating old pieces or redoing family heirlooms. Think a long time, however, before changing a piece of jewelry. Be sure you're not just momentarily tired of it. Styles do change, but some pieces are classics or may hold sentimental value.

One woman I know has a jade choker that is her favorite piece of jewelry. Though she probably has many more expensive pieces, this one was a gift from her mother. During the Great Depression, her mother had done some work for a small-town banker, who offered her a choice of three pieces of jewelry as payment for her services. She chose the most expensive one, a long jade rope, and years later she had it remade into three chokers, one for each of her daughters. In this case remaking a piece made the sentiment even more special.

In other instances, such as divorce, making an engagement or wedding ring into a necklace is often a happy solution to a sad problem. I have also seen many couples who married when they were of modest means, and wish to update their wedding bands to indicate their more current, affluent lifestyle.

Again, be certain changing the piece is what you want. Once done, it cannot be restored. The procedure for redoing an old piece is the same as ordering a new one.

Whether you buy in-stock or custom work, once you have bought a piece of fine jewelry, it's usually considered a final sale. It's not fair to the jeweler to take it back in a few weeks or days, complaining that it is not what you had in mind. The height of bad taste is to wear a piece to a social function, then try to return it shortly thereafter. Some jewelers occasionally lend their pieces to be worn at charity galas, obviously in exchange for the attention and publicity they will receive, but it's best not to think of your jeweler as you would your local lending library!

While most fine jewelers will not refund your money, unless, of course, there is something wrong with your purchase, they will often accept a piece for exchange towards a more expensive one. In this instance, jewelry is more flexible than many other consumer purchases. You can't actually get your money back after a year or two, but you can exchange the item and, by adding money to it, get something you like better.

Unlike most consumer items, the product sold by a jeweler literally lasts forever. Thus, if the jewelry is in good condition, the jeweler may be able to take the piece back, sell it again, or use the materials in other pieces. Who knows what fascinating histories lie behind the gems most of us wear every day?

Investing

Most people buy jewelry for one reason: pleasure. Whenever you buy exquisite, beautiful gems, you are making an investment in pleasure, akin to buying any fine art object. But, as with other art objects, there is also a profit to be made in the buying and selling of gems — if, and I stress that word, if — you know what you are doing.

Investing in gems is a complex subject, and without the necessary knowledge, it is possible — even probable — that you will be duped. As a jeweler, investing in gems is a topic I usually avoid because there is such a high degree of risk involved. It is a field best left to experts, and it is impossible to make anyone an expert in the space of these brief pages. And even experts cannot predict the whims or forces at work in the market.

For instance, in 1916, an American millionaire exchanged his house and land on Fifth Avenue in New York, valued at $925,000, for an extraordinary string of pearls, valued at $1 million. In 1956 the pearls, now made into two strands, were auctioned for prices of $90,000 and $61,000 — a drop in value of 83 percent. The drop was attributed to two factors: the introduction of cultured pearls and the increase in value of real estate in New York. Keep that example in mind whenever you hear about the rapid rise in gem values — there's always a high element of risk.

However anyone who collects fine jewelry undoubtedly has their interest piqued by the financial aspects of their purchases, and it's always helpful at least to be aware of the potential benefits and risks of any investment.

First, there is no such thing as a bad buy if you purchase truly beautiful, quality gems. Jewels are a limited commodity and have a centuries-old record of being valued by people around the world. In times of war, refugees have historically sewn loose stones into the linings of their clothes instead of currency, knowing that gems have a universal value. Thus, if you buy quality, your purchase is almost certain to hold its value and, in most cases, appreciate.

The biggest problem when investing in stones is liquidity. Like stocks, cars, art, or anything requiring a value judgment, just because someone appraises the item at a certain value, that does not necessarily mean there is someone willing to pay that price immediately at hand. For that reason, you should never invest in gems unless you have plenty of other liquid assets. It may take months or even years to sell a fine stone. If you cannot afford to wait for the right buyer, you cannot afford to be in the market.

Be prepared to hold stones for at least five years. You stand little chance of making a profit if you're unable to hold them that long. You may be able to break even before five years have passed, but your chances of making a profit are slim. It takes time for gems to increase in value — patience is requisite.

When buying as an investment, just as when you are buying stones for jewelry, it is crucial to deal only with a reputable jeweler. Avoid discounters or those who advertise promotional prices. Such dealers are usually less than stable and will prove difficult to build a longstanding relationship with during the time it takes to invest. Many reputable jewelers offer "buy back" guarantees, where they will purchase the stone back from you at a certain percentage of the original price. Always inquire about such policies, but as a rule of thumb, expect to get 90 percent as a reasonable buy back price.

Before buying any stone, I always recommend seeking a

second opinion. It is not insulting to the seller to ask for an independent appraisal or for you to ask to seek the advice of someone more knowledgeable. It's much better when making an investment as volatile as gems to be overly cautious.

The minimum investment required is $10,000. Any lower amount, in my opinion, rarely buys a gem of investment quality or size. For investment purposes, you must buy large stones. By large, I mean a carat or more. Smaller stones are simply not large enough to attract significant investor interest. An $800 diamond, for instance, has little resale value. There are thousands of such stones in the same size and quality range available at wholesale prices. For all the starry eyed young couples persuaded to buy engagement rings on the basis of investment, there are display cases full of lovely but small rings sitting in local pawn shops. Large stones are rare stones, and scarcity is what drives prices up.

My best advice is to concentrate on the rarest stones available. If I had unlimited funds to invest, I would put my money in colored diamonds or "fancies" because they are so rare.

I do not, however, recommend buying diamonds per se. The market is carefully controlled by the DeBeers company, which manipulates supply and demand through persuasive advertising. But even the DeBeers monopoly is threatened by a flood of diamonds from Russia, and by the political instability in South Africa. Prices are currently dipping in the diamond market, and while the stones will always be valued, fine examples of other stones make better investment bets.

Besides colored diamonds, I would stick to the rest of the Big Four: rubies, sapphires, and emeralds. Other valuable stones are more subject to changing tastes and may quickly fall from favor before you could liquidate your holdings.

When buying investment stones, a GIA certificate describing the stones is mandatory. Such a certificate will give only the quality of the stone, not a value, so an appraisal from your jeweler is also necessary.

Most investors, once they have purchased stones, place them in a vault and leave them there untouched. That's perfectly acceptable; but as a lover of fine stones, I hate to see any beautiful object hidden from sight. With proper insurance and care, it's also perfectly acceptable and safe to have the stone mounted and worn. The gem can always be removed from its setting for sale, and you get the added benefit of enjoying your investment. That's certainly more than can be said for a certificate of deposit or a blue chip stock!

When you are ready to sell the stone, know that most jewelers act on consignment almost exclusively. Unless they have agreed to buy it back from you, they will offer to sell it on your behalf, usually for a commission of 10 to 20 percent of the purchase price.

If you do succeed in buying and selling stones for profit as well as pleasure, you'll undoubtedly want to continue. But no matter how long you're in the business of investing in gems, remember it involves great care, patience, and risk.

I have never yet seen anyone who didn't enjoy the added lift one receives from wearing a beautiful gem. The jewelry, if chosen to complement the wearer's assets and clothing, always adds that special something that makes people sit up and take notice. It's called style, and it's something the world needs more of. Style doesn't cost a great deal of money but it does take time and effort. As anyone who has ever marveled at the gifts of nature and the art of mankind knows, it's an expenditure well worthwhile, and best of all, one that results in great joy and fun.

GLOSSARY

Asterism: The appearance of white lines in the shape of a star, present in some sapphires and rubies when cut en cabochon.

Baguette: A small rectangularly shaped diamond, used in groups, to set off larger gems.

Bangle: A stiff, circular bracelet.

Cabochon or en cabochon: A domed, unfaceted style of cutting, used primarily for opaque stones.

Choker: A short necklace fitting close to the neck, usually made of bulky materials.

Carat: A unit of weight used for stones, equal to 200 milligrams or 1/5 gram.

Clarity: Term used to indicate the absence of internal flaws.

Clip-ons: Earrings which adhere to the lobe through the use of adjustable backs, rather than posts which pierce the ear.

Color: Term used to indicate the shade of a diamond.

Cut: The shape a stone takes when transformed from a rough stone to a gem.

Fancies: Extremely rare, naturally colored diamonds.

Flexible: Bracelet made of chainlike links, fastened with a clasp.

Karat: Term used to indicate the purity of gold.

Matinee: Single strand necklace measuring about 20 to 24 inches long.

Opera: Single strand necklace measuring about 28 to 30 inches long.

Pave: To cover the surface with many tiny diamonds placed closely together.

Plunging clasp: Type of fastener with tiny hooks that hold two ends of a necklace or bracelet together, and which is usually hidden.

Point: Diamond weight measurement for stones under 1 carat. 100 points equal one carat.

Riviere: A single strand necklace of diamond solitaires formed into a necklace; literally means "river."

Rope: A necklace measuring 45 to 120 inches long.

Spring ring: A small circle with a movable latch which holds two ends of a bracelet or necklace together.

Acknowledgements

The author would like to thank Lou Lattimore, Tanya Blair Agency, Kim Dawson Agency, and Page Parkes Models Rep.

Special thanks to Mr. Laurence Graff for his generous contribution of photos.

The publisher would like to thank Kim Robbins for her contributions as stylist and hair and make-up artist on the fashion photography.